HISTORY OF THE GREAT WAR

MILITARY OPERATIONS

HISTORY OF THE GREAT WAR

BASED ON OFFICIAL DOCUMENTS

BY DIRECTION OF THE HISTORICAL SECTION OF THE
COMMITTEE OF IMPERIAL DEFENCE

MILITARY OPERATIONS

FRANCE AND BELGIUM, 1917

THE GERMAN RETREAT TO THE HINDENBURG LINE AND
THE BATTLES OF ARRAS

APPENDICES

MACMILLAN AND CO., LIMITED
ST. MARTIN'S STREET, LONDON
1940

COPYRIGHT

PRINTED IN GREAT BRITAIN
BY R. & R. CLARK, LIMITED, EDINBURGH

PREFACE

THE documents in this volume have reference to the Allied plans of campaign for the year 1917, and particularly to the change of plans occasioned by the supersession of General Joffre by General Nivelle ; to the important Allied Conference held at Calais on the 26th-27th February 1917 ; and to the plans and preparations for the Battles of Arras and of Bullecourt, including the tactical instructions, G.H.Q. and Army orders, and specimen corps, divisional, infantry brigade and artillery instructions.

NOTE.—Localities indicated by map co-ordinates according to the system in vogue in 1917 are identified wherever necessary.

MAPS

(In Separate Case)

TABLE OF APPENDICES

RESOLUTIONS OF THE CHANTILLY CONFERENCE ·

(TRANSLATION)

16th November 1916.

Decisions reached by the Commanders-in-Chief of the Allied Armies or their accredited representatives at the conclusion of the Conference held at Chantilly, on the 15th and 16th November 1916.

I. The Conference gives its approval to the plan of action of the Coalition, as laid down in the Memorandum submitted to it. This plan has as its object the endowment of the campaigns of 1917 with a decisive character.

It adopts, in consequence, the following resolutions :—

(a) During the winter 1916–1917 the offensive operations now in course will be continued in such measure as the climatic conditions of each front render possible.

(b) In order to be as far as possible in a position to meet any unforeseen situation, and especially to prevent the enemy from in any respect regaining the initiative, the Armies of the Coalition will be ready to undertake general offensives from the first fortnight of February 1917 with all the means at their disposal.

(c) From the moment when the Armies are ready to attack, the Commanders-in-Chief will take action in accordance with the situation then prevailing on their respective fronts.

(d) If circumstances do not forbid, the general offensives, in the maximum strength that each Army can put in the field, will be launched on all fronts at the earliest moment at which they can be synchronized,[1] on dates which will be fixed by agreement between the Commanders-in-Chief.

(e) In order to ensure the necessary agreement in these different cases, the Commanders-in-Chief will maintain an unceasing and close contact.

II. On the Balkan Front :—

(a) The Coalition will seek to put Bulgaria out of action as soon as possible. It is the intention of the Russian Command to continue and intensify with this end in view the operations already in course.

---

[1] This condition of synchronization may be considered to have been fulfilled if the period between the launch of the offensives on the different fronts does not exceed three weeks.

(*b*) Against Bulgaria the Russo-Rumanian forces will act from the north and the Allied Army of Salonika from the south, the actions of these two groups of forces being closely combined in order to obtain a decision on one front or the other, in accordance with the development of the operations.

(*c*) The Allied Army of the East will be raised as soon as possible to a strength of 23 divisions ; this strength corresponds on the one hand with the number of troops which it is possible to handle and to supply in the theatre of operations in view, and on the other, with the reinforcements which it is possible to withdraw from the western theatres of operations. In order to attain this strength the British Government will without delay increase their forces to seven divisions, and the French Government theirs to six divisions ; the Italian Government will be made acquainted with the strongly-expressed intentions of the Russian High Command and will be requested to increase to three divisions the Italian contingent at Salonika.

(*d*) The Allied Army of the East will be carefully maintained at full strength.

III.   Secondary Theatres of Operations.

On all the secondary fronts actions intended to immobilize the forces of the enemy will be carried out with means as restricted as possible, in order to reserve the maximum forces for the principal theatres.

IV.   Mutual Support.

(*a*) The Conference renews the undertaking of mutual support, given at the Conference of the 5th December 1915 and fully observed by all throughout the present year, that is :

If one Power is attacked, the others will come immediately to its aid to the full limit of their resources, either indirectly, by attacks which Armies not themselves assailed by the enemy will launch on fronts previously decided on, or directly, by the despatch of forces where theatres of operations are linked by easy communications.

(*b*) In order to be prepared for this latter eventuality, questions of transportation and of the employment of mixed forces will be studied by the Franco-British and Italian General Staffs.

V.   Maintenance of the Effectives of the Serbian Army.

The effective strength of the Serbian Army will be kept up by means of the voluntary enrolment of prisoners of Serbian race in the hands of Italy and Russia, to the full measure and with all the precautions considered necessary by these two Powers.

Signed by the Representatives of the Commanders-in-Chief of the Allied Armies present at the Conference and designated below :—

> For Belgium :

General Wielemans, Chief of the General Staff of
  the Belgian Army .   .   .   .   . WIELEMANS.

> For Great Britain :

General Sir William Robertson, Chief of the Imperial General Staff of the British Armies   . W. ROBERTSON.
General Sir Douglas Haig, Commander-in-Chief of
  the British Armies in France   .   .   . D. HAIG.

For Italy :

General Porro, Chief of the General Staff of the
Italian Army [1] . . . . . PORRO.

For Rumania :

Colonel Rudeanu, Chief of the Rumanian Military
Mission to the French G.Q.G. . . . RUDEANU.

For Russia :

General Palitzine, Representative of H.M. the Tsar,
Commander-in-Chief of the Russian Troops, and
Chief of the Russian Military Mission . . PALITZINE.

For Serbia :

General Rachitch, Delegate of the Serbian Army
to the French G.Q.G. . . . . RACHITCH.

For France :

General Joffre, Commander-in-Chief of the French
Armies . . . . . . J. JOFFRE.

[1] He was actually Sub-Chief [Compiler's Note].

LETTER No. 17856/3, FROM GENERAL NIVELLE TO GENERAL SIR DOUGLAS HAIG, 21st DECEMBER 1916

(Translation)

My dear General,
    In continuation of our conversation on the 20th December, I have the honour to set out below my views on the subject of our offensive of 1917 and of the modifications which I consider necessary in the original plan of these operations.

Objective.—In the offensive of 1917 the Franco-British Armies must strive to destroy the main body of the enemy's Armies on the Western Front.   This result can be attained only after a decisive battle, with considerable superiority of numbers, against all the available forces of the enemy.

It is therefore necessary :
    —to pin down as large a proportion as possible of the hostile forces ;
    —to break the enemy's front in such a manner that the rupture can be immediately exploited ;
    —to overcome all the reserves with which our adversary can oppose us ;
    —to exploit with all our resources the result of this decisive battle.

Resources required.—In order to carry out this programme it is essential to have the disposal of a mass of manœuvre sufficiently strong to overcome without chance of failure all the hostile reserves available, in addition to the forces required at the beginning to pin down the enemy and break his front.
    I consider that this mass should be a homogeneous force possessing full cohesion and trained for its task by the commanders who will have to make use of it.   It follows that this force cannot be drawn from the Armies entrusted with a wearing-down offensive or with the rupture of the enemy's front.
    I put the necessary strength of this mass of manœuvre at a group of 3 Armies, each of 3 corps of 3 divisions.

General Aspect of the Operations.—Starting from these foundations, I envisage the development of the operations of our Armies as follows.

The enemy's forces will be pinned down in the area Arras—Bapaume and in that between Oise and Somme by attacks conducted respectively by the Armies under your orders and by French forces.

At the same time an *attaque brusquée* carried out on another part of the French front will bring about the break-through. This will be followed immediately by the rapid enlargement of the breach and the concentration beyond it of the Armies of manœuvre destined for the decisive battle.

This battle, the effects of which cannot fail to make themselves felt over the whole extent of our front, will consist of an extremely vigorous exploitation in which the French and British Armies will participate with all the resources at their disposal.

Constitution of the Mass of Manœuvre.—The success of our operations depends then essentially upon the mass of manœuvre.

For reasons which I have already pointed out to you (homogeneity, cohesion, training, command) I consider that this force should be distinct from the higher formations entrusted with the attack north of the Oise and the execution of the break-through.

Now it is impossible, having regard to the present distribution of the front between our allied Armies, for me to form this reserve of 27 divisions.

In order to permit me to do so, it is absolutely necessary that the British Armies should relieve a considerable proportion of the French troops holding the front between Somme and Oise and that they should thereby render available the French divisions now between Bouchavesnes and the road from Amiens to Roye. I consider that this front can easily be held by 7 or 8 divisions, which would correspond to the density of the German forces facing it.

This relief must be carried out without any delay, or the preparations for our coming operation will be seriously retarded ; I therefore ask you to have it carried out by the 15th January at latest.

Rôle of the British Armies.—In sum, the rôle of the British Armies in our joint offensive should be :

1. To permit me to form without delay the mass of manœuvre which is indispensable for the decisive battle ;

2. To undertake on the front of attack which you have in mind an offensive sufficiently large and powerful to absorb a considerable proportion of the German reserves ;

(I consider that your front of attack should have a breadth of 30 to 40 kilometres, according to whether or not you are disposed to leave passive sectors in it.)

3. To participate in the general exploitation which will follow the decisive battle in another area by bringing about the disorganization of the forces in position opposite your front and by undertaking the pursuit of the enemy within a zone on which we can decide later by common accord.

In thus defining the task of the British Armies I desire to make clear to you that I am also considering the possible employment of my mass of manœuvre on the right flank of our front.

Should the enemy attempt an offensive through Switzerland, I should thus not be compelled to call upon you to put at my disposition part of your forces to oppose it.

It is also evident that this group of Armies held in reserve will in the general engagement be acting for the benefit of your Armies as well as of mine.

Besides, the extension of your front which I am demanding will to a certain extent relieve your Armies from the execution of the offensive operations which they were to have undertaken in the course of the winter in accordance with the decisions reached at the Chantilly Conference of the 15th November last.

Finally, the plan which I have put before you does not exclude the possibility of carrying out, in case of need, the operation for the capture of Ostend and Zeebrugge, since that cannot take place until the summer.

This operation can be considered in all its details in the light of the directive already adopted, and I even think that our Belgian allies ought to prepare from now onward for the rôle they will have to assume in it.

If our grand offensive succeeds, it is certain that the Belgian coast will fall into our hands as a result of the retreat of the German Armies and without direct attack.

If, on the contrary, our attacks fail, it will still be possible to carry out in the fine weather the operations projected in Flanders.

In concluding this explanation, I ask you to be good enough to let me have as soon as possible your answer on the subject of the relief of the front between Bouchavesnes and the Roye road ; the constitution of my reserves in view of the varied eventualities which may arise is, indeed, a question of capital importance and one to which I want to find the solution without any delay.

Accept, my dear General, the expression of my
most cordial sentiments,
R. NIVELLE.

TELEGRAM FROM FRENCH MILITARY MISSION BRITISH G.H.Q. TO FRENCH G.Q.G., 23RD DECEMBER 1916

(TRANSLATION)

E. M. Montreuil [1] to G.Q.G. (3rd Bureau)
Nos. 2395 and 2396.

In reply to your letter No. 17856 from General Nivelle, General Haig made this morning the following statement :

First.—French Command's demand requires employment 10 British divisions ; there would then remain only 8 divisions in reserve, 6 of them of very mediocre value.

Second.—General Haig cannot accept in the present circumstances a situation which would deprive his Armies of all offensive capacity.

Third.—He has therefore brought the question before British War Committee, asking it to send France divisions necessary to satisfy French Command's demand.

Fourth.—He is insistently demanding return division from Salonika.

Fifth.—The relief could be begun in a fortnight from now and continued as fresh divisions arrived, if sent.

Sixth.—It is to be expected that British General Staff will raise difficulties as to extending front to south of road Amiens, Péronne, wishing to keep in hand reserves for offensive action.

[1] E[tat] M[ajor] Montreuil stands for the French Military Mission to British G.H.Q. For a comment upon this telegram see p. 40 footnote 2.

LETTER FROM THE COMMANDER-IN-CHIEF BRITISH ARMIES IN FRANCE TO THE COMMANDER - IN - CHIEF FRENCH ARMIES OF THE NORTH AND NORTH-EAST

25th December 1916.

O.A.D. 285

My dear General,

I beg to acknowledge receipt of your letter No. 17,856 of the 21st December 1916, which has had my very careful consideration.

I agree in principle with your proposals and am desirous of doing all that I can to help you on the lines you suggest. The extent to which I can help, however, depends on the number of divisions sent to me within the next two or three months from Salonika and elsewhere, and at present I have no definite information on this point. I am in communication with Sir William Robertson on the subject and will inform you exactly what I can do as soon as I learn from him what divisions will be sent to me and when they will arrive. In the meantime all that I can undertake to do is to relieve your troops as far as the Amiens—Villers Bretonneux—St. Quentin road, commencing on the first February, provided, of course, that there is no diminution of the forces under my orders. I regret that I cannot possibly commence the relief at an earlier date than that.

Yours very truly,

D. HAIG,

General.

APPENDIX 5.

LETTER FROM THE CHIEF OF THE IMPERIAL GENERAL STAFF TO THE FIELD - MARSHAL COMMANDING - IN - CHIEF BRITISH ARMIES IN FRANCE

1st January 1917.

0.1/68/210.

With reference to your O.A.D. 256 of the 25th December 1916, in view of the great importance which the War Cabinet attach, as you are aware, to the capture of Ostend and Zeebrugge before next winter, I shall be glad if you will inform me whether, in your opinion, General Nivelle's plan of operations and the proposed extension of your front is likely to prevent you from undertaking the operations which you contemplate in Belgium.

W. R. ROBERTSON,
General,
C.I.G.S.

NOTE.—In reply, on the 6th January, Sir Douglas Haig forwarded a copy of his letter to General Nivelle which is given in Appendix 7, remarking that it would show how the matter stood. He also stated how urgent it was that further divisions should be sent out to him, in order that he might take over to the Amiens-Roye road and thus fully support General Nivelle's plans.

G.H.Q. LETTER O.A.D. 258,
2ND JANUARY 1917

To

General Sir H. S. Horne, K.C.B.,
    Commanding First Army.
General Sir H. C. O. Plumer, G.C.M.G., K.C.B.,
    Commanding Second Army.
General Sir E. H. H. Allenby, K.C.B.,
    Commanding Third Army.
General Sir H. S. Rawlinson, Bt., K.C.B., K.C.V.O.,
    Commanding Fourth Army.
General Sir H. de la P. Gough, K.C.B.,
    Commanding Fifth Army.
Lieut.-General C. T. McM. Kavanagh, K.C.B., C.V.O., D.S.O.,
    Commanding Cavalry Corps.

1. The general plan upon which the operations of 1917 will be based is as follows :—

The French will withdraw the maximum number of their troops into reserve with a view to the delivery of a decisive attack on a large scale. In order to give this attack the best chance of success subsidiary attacks will be made north of the River Oise by French and British troops.

The British attacks will be carried out in the Ancre Valley, opposite Arras, and against the Vimy Ridge by the Fifth, Third, and First Armies respectively.

The object of these attacks will be :—

(a) To take full advantage of the favourable situation which already exists in the pronounced enemy's salient west of Bapaume by destroying or capturing the hostile forces in that salient.

(b) To pin the enemy to his ground, draw in his reserves, and thereby facilitate the task of the main French attack.

2. In view of the above, the Commander-in-Chief has decided :—

(i) to relieve the French troops on the right of the British Army as far south as the Amiens—Villers Bretonneux—St. Quentin road (inclusive to the British) ;

(ii) to push forward as quickly as possible all preparations for offensive operations on the Ancre, Arras, and Vimy fronts, so that, should necessity arise, these operations can be undertaken at the earliest possible date.

3.   The Fourth Army will extend its right as far south as the Villers Bretonneux road in the following manner :—

To the Quarry Farm, relief commencing on 15th January 1917.
To the River Somme, relief commencing on 25th January 1917.
To the Villers Bretonneux Road, relief commencing on 1st February 1917.

A conference with the French will be assembled at an early date at Fourth Army Headquarters, at which the new boundary lines and other details of relief will be arranged.

After the relief has been completed the Fourth Army should aim at maintaining four divisions in Reserve.

It is not the intention of the Commander-in-Chief that offensive operations on a large scale shall be undertaken by the Fourth Army. This Army will, however, make all necessary arrangements to carry out limited operations in order to induce the enemy to believe that the battle of the Somme is recommencing.

4.   The attack of the Fifth Army will be made in the direction of Achiet le Grand.   It will be undertaken by successive advances. Each advance is to be thoroughly prepared and to be carried out with due regard to the necessity for economy of personnel.   It is to be realized that the Fourth Army will not be in a position to undertake any serious offensive operation and will only maintain touch with the right of the Fifth Army.

The Fifth Army will be prepared to take advantage of any considerable success gained by the Third Army by pressing forward in the direction of Achiet le Grand.

5.   The Third Army will attack the enemy astride the River Scarpe on a front from Beaurains (inclusive) to Roclincourt, in accordance with the plan of operations already submitted.

The objectives of the Third Army will be :—

Firstly, to seize the high ground about Monchy le Preux.
Secondly, to turn the German defences south of Arras by a rapid
  advance in a south-easterly direction towards Croisilles and
  Bullecourt.

The Cavalry Corps (less 2 Divisions) will be placed at the disposal of the Third Army for the purpose of these operations.

6.   The First Army will attack the Vimy Ridge simultaneously with the attack by the Third Army with the object of :—

(a) securing the northern flank of the Third Army attack ;
(b) gaining observation over the Douai Plain.

The necessary readjustment of boundary lines between the First and Third Armies will be made, and orders on this subject will be issued at an early date.

7.   The schemes which have already been submitted by Armies will shortly be returned, together with any remarks which may be necessary regarding the scope, object, and execution of each operation and any amendments or adjustments which may be required.

Revised schemes will be submitted by each army on the 31st January.

8. A revised statement of troops, guns, ammunition, and other resources will also be issued shortly.

Briefly, the ultimate allotment of divisions to each army, so far as can be forecast at present, is as follows :—

First Army	. .	10 divisions
Second Army	. .	10 ,,
Third Army	. .	18 ,,
Fourth Army	. .	12 ,,
Fifth Army	. .	12 ,,

Total 62 divisions

9. Instructions regarding the dumping of ammunition will be issued at an early date.

10. On receipt of the above information and instructions Armies will at once revise their transportation requirements in conjunction with their A.D.'s Tn.

L. E. KIGGELL,
Lieut.-General,
Chief of the General Staff.

LETTER O.A.D. 262, FROM FIELD-MARSHAL SIR DOUGLAS HAIG TO GENERAL NIVELLE, 6TH JANUARY 1917

My dear General,

I beg to acknowledge receipt of your letters No. 23139, dated the 27th December 1916, No. 655, dated the 1st January 1917, and No. 1005, dated the 2nd January 1917, on the subject of the plan of operations which we have already discussed, and the proposed relief of French troops by British.

I will deal first with the plan of operations, on which the solution of all minor problems depends. It is essential that there should be no room for misunderstanding between us on this question.

In your letter of the 2nd January you divide the operations into three phases.

In the first phase you propose that strong attacks shall be made by our respective armies with the object not only of drawing in and using up the enemy's reserves, but of gaining such tactical successes as will open the way for decisive action on the fronts of attack, either immediately, or—later on—as a result of success obtained by you in the second phase. During this first phase adequate reserves are to be held ready either to exploit success immediately, or to continue to use up the enemy's reserves, according to the development of the situation.

I have already agreed to launch such an attack as you describe, but not to an indefinite continuation of the battle to use up the enemy's reserves. Such continuation might result in a prolonged struggle, like that on the Somme this year, and would be contrary to our agreement that we must seek a definite and rapid decision.

In the second phase you propose that my offensive shall be continued while you seek a decision on another front. This I have also agreed to on the definite understanding that your decisive attack will be launched within a short period—about eight to fourteen days—after the commencement of the first phase ; and, further, that the second phase also will be of very short duration. You will remember that you estimated a period of 24 to 48 hours as sufficient to enable you to decide whether your decisive attack had succeeded or should be abandoned.

The third phase, as described in your letter of the 2nd January, will consist in the exploitation by the French and British Armies of the successes previously gained. This is, of course, on the assumption that the previous successes have been of such magnitude as will make it reasonably certain that by following them up at once we can gain a complete victory and, at least, force the enemy to abandon the Belgian coast. On that assumption I agree also to the third phase on the general lines described in your letter.

But I must make it quite clear that my concurrence in your plan is absolutely limited by the considerations I have explained above, on which we have already agreed in our conversations on the subject. It is essential that the Belgian coast shall be cleared this summer. I hope and believe that we shall be able to effect much more than that, and within limitations of time I will cooperate to the utmost of my power in the larger plans which you have proposed.

But it must distinctly be understood between us that if I am not satisfied that this larger plan, as events develop, promises the degree of success necessary to clear the Belgian coast, then I not only cannot continue the battle but I will look to you to fulfil the undertaking you have given me verbally to relieve on the defensive front the troops I require for my northern offensive.

In short, the first two phases of the battle cannot be of " une durée prolongée ", as you suggest on the first page of your letter of the 2nd January. If these two phases are not so successful as to justify me in entering on the third phase, then I must transfer my main forces to the north. To enable me to do this in sufficient time to carry out my plans it would be necessary that the relief of the troops on the southern part of my front should be carried out by the middle of June. Moreover, to give me sufficient force to carry out the northern attack, I should ask you to take over my front up to the Ancre Valley.

Thus, there is, in fact, a fourth phase of the battle to be provided for in our plans. The need to carry it out may not, and, I hope, will not, arise. But the clearance of the Belgian coast is of such importance to the British Government that it must be fully provided for before I can finally agree to your proposals.

In our conversations you have already agreed in principle to these stipulations, and I shall be obliged if you will now inform me, after fuller consideration, that you can definitely accept them.

In this connection I beg that you will give full consideration to the question of what is the greatest extent of front on which you could relieve my troops if the need should arise, and if there should be a doubt of your being able to take over as far as the Ancre I beg that the possibility of obtaining the help of Italian troops may be carefully examined.

As regards the relief of your troops on my present right, subject to our final agreement on the plan of operations I have given orders that it is to commence on the 15th January, and I am arranging with the G.A.N. for a meeting to be held with representatives of my Fourth Army on Sunday next to settle details.

I calculate that it should be possible to complete the relief as far as the Villers Bretonneux Road about the 15th February.

I trust that I have already made it clear to you that I cannot relieve your troops to the south of that road unless a larger number of divisions are sent to me than have so far been promised.

For my operations, in cooperation with you, on the Bapaume—Vimy front I require not less than 35 divisions. On my defensive front, to the Villers Bretonneux Road I cannot do with less than 27 Divisions until active operations are on the point of commencing. This makes a total of 62, of which I have at present only 56. I expect two more from England this month and have been told that it is probable, but not certain, that I shall receive two in February and another in April, besides one Portuguese division.

No hope of any beyond these has been held out to me so far. I am again writing to the War Office on the subject.

In regard to the date of the allied offensive, it was agreed at the last Conference of Commanders-in-Chief that the allies should be prepared to attack by the date mentioned in your letter of the 27th December if circumstances should render it necessary to do so. At the same time, however, I pointed out that my Armies could not be ready to attack in full force before the 1st May, and both the Russian and Italian representatives were also in favour of this later date.

It was recognized that it is of great importance that all the allies should attack practically simultaneously and in the greatest force possible, and personally I hold that view very strongly. Circumstances may compel us to take offensive action, with such forces as can be made available, before we are all fully ready ; but we must regard it as a grave disadvantage if this should occur and we must strive to avoid it. We have evidence that the enemy fears the results of combined simultaneous action by the allies in full force. We must expect him to take steps intended to prevent such combination, and we must beware of being deceived into complying with his intentions by launching attacks prematurely on any one front, or even on all.

Yours very truly,

D. HAIG,
Field-Marshal.

LONDON CONVENTION OF
16TH JANUARY 1917
(TRANSLATION)

As a result of the conference held in London on the 15th January 1917, the following agreement has been reached between Field-Marshal Haig and General Nivelle :—

1. The British Armies will continue the relief of the French forces south of Genermont [1] as far as the Amiens—Roye road in such a manner that this operation shall be completed by the first week of March.[2]

2. The British and French Armies will take the offensive at latest on the 1st April and before that date if it is possible or if the general situation requires it, in conformity with the decisions reached at the Chantilly Conference on the 15th November 1916.

3. This offensive will conform in execution to the plan drawn up with the approval of Field-Marshal Haig and explained by General Nivelle to the conference on the 15th January.

4. The exploitation of the successes obtained on the three fronts of attack will be carried out with the full vigour necessary to obtain a decisive result and by means of the employment, if required, of all the available reserves of the British and French Armies.

5. In case these operations do not achieve the success which is expected and which ought to be very rapidly attained, the battle will be broken off by agreement, in order to allow the British Armies to engage in other operations on a front further north, in co-operation with the Belgian Army and with the French Nieuport Group.

6. These arrangements, which conform to the directives given by the French War Committee to General Nivelle, have been approved by the British War Committee, which will facilitate

---

[1] Genermont is a hamlet south of the Amiens—St. Quentin road, half-way along the then front line between that road at Villers-Carbonnel and the town of Chaulnes. At a conference held at the headquarters of the British Fourth Army at Querrieu, on the 7th January, it had been decided that the relief thus far should be carried out by the 16th February. It actually began on the 16th January, the day this agreement was signed, and was completed by the 13th February.

[2] In the copy retained by Sir Douglas Haig the words " le 15 février " are erased and replaced by " la première semaine de mars ".

their execution as far as possible in respect of the means to be put at the disposal of Field-Marshal Haig.

7. They will not be modified except in the case of an offensive on the part of the enemy on another part of the Western Front necessitating the intervention of the main body of the French Armies in this new theatre of operations.

8. In such a case the British Armies would give them all the assistance in their power by attacking with all the means at their disposal on their present front, or by such other action as the circumstances suggested, by agreement between the two Commanders-in-Chief.

D. HAIG, F.M. R. NIVELLE.
16 Jan : 17.

W. R. ROBERTSON, General,
16/1/17.

G.H.Q. LETTER O.A.D. 286,
26TH JANUARY 1917

To

First Army.
Second Army.
Third Army.
Fourth Army.
Fifth Army.
Cavalry Corps.

With reference to O.A.D. 258, dated the 2nd January.

1. Further communications have been held with the French regarding the general plan of operations on the Western Front, with the result that the Field-Marshal Commanding-in-Chief has decided to take over the front and relieve the French troops as far south as the Amiens—Roye road by the end of February.

It is anticipated that some additional British divisions will be sent to France and there is no intention to alter materially the fronts or scope of the attacks to be carried out by the British as described in the paper mentioned above, i.e.,

The Ancre valley attack by the Fifth Army.
The Scarpe valley attack by the Third Army.
The Vimy ridge attack by the First Army.

2. In order to give effect to the above the following redistribution of troops will take place :—

The 3rd Division will be transferred (about 1st February) from the Fifth Army to the Third Army.

The 34th Division will be transferred (about 6th February) from the Second Army to the Third Army.

The 57th Division will be posted on arrival (early in February) to the Second Army.

The 35th Division will be transferred (about 7th February) from the Third Army to the Fourth Army.

The 51st Division will be transferred (about 6th February) from the Fifth Army to the Third Army.

The Headquarters and Corps Troops, IV Corps and the 61st Division will be transferred (about the second week in February) from the Fifth Army to the Fourth Army.

The 32nd or 62nd Division will be transferred (about the second week in February) from the Fifth Army to the Fourth Army.

The I Anzac Corps (1A, 2A, 4A, 5A) and front will be transferred on February 15th from the Fourth Army to the Fifth Army.

" A " Territorial Division will be posted on arrival (about 16th February) and " C " Territorial Division on arrival (in March) to the Fourth Army, and will each release a division to be transferred to the Third Army.

The Portuguese Division will be posted on arrival (in February) to the First Army and will release a division to be transferred to the Third Army.

" B " Territorial Division and 5th Canadian Division } will be posted on arrival (in March) to the First Army, releasing two divisions to be transferred to the Third Army.

3. The following will be the distribution of Corps and Divisions between Armies :—

(a) The Fourth Army will consist of III, IV, XIV, and XV Corps (15 divisions) and will hold the front from the Amiens —Roye road to the present left of the XIV Corps. At least three divisions will, in the first instance, be kept in reserve. In March two more divisions will be brought into reserve. The number of divisions will be reduced from 15 to 12, as shown on the attached table.

(b) The Fifth Army will consist of II, V, XIII, and I Anzac Corps (12 divisions).

It is intended to increase this number of divisions to 14 prior to the commencement of operations.

(c) The Third Army will consist of VI, VII, XVII, XVIII, and XIX Corps (10 divisions).

It is intended to increase the number of divisions in this Army gradually to 18 prior to the commencement of operations.

Of these, one Corps of three divisions will be held in G.H.Q. Reserve.

(d) The First Army will consist of the Canadian, I, and XI Corps (10 divisions).

This number of divisions will be maintained.

(e) The Second Army will consist of VIII, IX, X, and II Anzac Corps (12 divisions).

This number of divisions will be reduced to 10 prior to the commencement of operations.

A Table is attached showing the changes proposed.

4. The forecast of the allotment of artillery resources issued with O.A.D. 274, dated the 10th January, para. 6 (a) and (b), remains unaltered as regards Heavy and Siege Artillery, but the figures for 18-pdr. guns and 4·5″ howitzers should be amended as follows :—

		First Army.	Third Army.	Fifth Army.
Maximum	18-pdr.	666	1,080	720
	4·5″ how.	198	330	216
Minimum	18-pdr.	654	828	702
	4·5″ how.	198	300	216

5. The movements of divisions, etc., outlined in the preceding paragraphs cannot be completed in time for the full plan of operations to be put into effect before about the 15th March, by which date, at the latest, the Commander-in-Chief looks to Army Commanders to have everything in readiness to commence the attack.

He desires to remind Army Commanders, however, that this date applies only to the full plan of operations and that, in accordance with the instructions given by him at the Conference held at the Third Army Headquarters on the 18th November 1916 (O.A.D. 291/19), it may be necessary to undertake an offensive, with as strong forces as can be made available, at any time after the 1st February. It is necessary that preparations for such an offensive shall be completed accordingly.

L. E. KIGGELL,
Lieut.-General,
Chief of the General Staff.

FIFTH ARMY LETTER S.G. 235 TO G.H.Q., 30TH JANUARY 1917

In accordance with the instructions contained in your O.A.D. 261 of the 2nd January, the plan of Fifth Army Operations has been modified in accordance with O.A.D. 258 of the 2nd January, and is now re-submitted.

Possible action by the 1st Anzac Corps is not at present included in the definite scheme, as that Corps is not yet under Fifth Army orders. That question is, however, under consideration (see para. 3 (*d*)) and a further plan will be forwarded if desired by you.

2.   The objective given to the Fifth Army is Achiet-le-Grand.   To reach that place, or Achiet-le-Petit, it will be necessary to secure the flanks of any advance by the capture of Serre and Bois Loupart. The earlier operations of the Fifth Army will therefore be directed towards securing those two points.   It is hardly possible at this moment to forecast anything beyond these preliminary movements.

3.   The strength of the Fifth Army available for these operations will be 10 divisions, exclusive of the Anzac Corps.

With a view to economizing personnel and making the best use of the guns under my command, the advance towards Bois Loupart will take place in four stages as shown on the accompanying map.

Those stages, and the approximate dates, will be as follows :—

(*a*)   To be carried out by the II Corps (63rd Division) on the 3rd February :—Capture of Pusieux Trench and River Trench from their Southern ends as far North as the junctions with Artillery Alley and Swan Trench.

This will enable the V Corps to extend its right and to get a better position for the attack upon Serre.

(*b*)   To be carried out by the II Corps, 20th February :—Establish ourselves firmly on Hill 130, South of Miraumont.   Capture Grandcourt Trench and Tea Trench from the South, while the 63rd Division North of the R. Ancre takes Baillescourt Farm and the Hollow Road running North towards Puisieux.

This will have the effect of cutting off Grandcourt and its garrison without actually attacking that village.

(*c*)   To be carried out by the V Corps, 20th March :—The capture of Serre together with the trenches to the East and South-East, i.e. Pendant Alley East, Puisieux Trench, River Trench as far North as L.26.c.4.7.

C

(*d*) To be carried out by both Corps, 25th March :—Capture
of Pys, Miraumont and Beauregard Dovecote.

If possible this attack will be combined with another by
the 1st Anzac Corps which will have as its object the capture
of Little Wood and the Butte de Warlencourt. This operation cannot yet be definitely decided upon.

4. When the above operations have been brought to a successful
conclusion, the Fifth Army will be favourably placed for an attack
upon Bois Loupart, which will be carried out as quickly as possible.
Further operations must depend upon what progress is made elsewhere.

5. The distribution of my force will be as follows :—

(*a*) Anzac Corps : 1st, 2nd, 3rd, 4th Anzac Divisions.

(*b*) II Corps : 2nd, 18th, 63rd Divisions. One division to come
from the Fourth Army.

(*c*) V Corps : 7th, 11th, 19th, 62nd Divisions.

(*d*) XIII Corps : 31st Division.

(*e*) Army Reserve : The last division to arrive from the Fourth
Army.

6. I would request that I may be provided with my allotment of
Special Brigade, R.E. not later than the 1st March, as I propose,
if possible, to make great use of Livens Projectors for the attack
upon Serre.

I should also be very glad if Captain Livens, M.C., could be
placed at my disposal, as he has already an intimate knowledge of
the ground.[1]

I would like to point out that up to the 1st April we shall be
short of about 2 Brigades working under the orders of the Transportation Dept. I should, of course, be very glad if they could be
relieved by 15th March.

H. P. GOUGH,
General,
Commanding Fifth Army.

---

[1] The Livens Projector, with a maximum range of 1,200–1,400 yards,
was fired electrically in salvoes of fifteen. It fired drums containing each
30 lbs. of lethal gas, so that an enormous quantity could be projected by
the simultaneous discharge of a number of batches of projectors. Captain
Livens was the inventor.

BATTLES OF ARRAS
PLAN OF OPERATIONS FOR FIRST ARMY

1.   The task of the First Army is to form a strong defensive flank
for the operations of the Third Army by the capture of the Vimy
Ridge (from the Commandant's House to the Pimple) and Thélus,
and to obtain the observation over the Douai plain.

The capture of the Vimy Ridge and particularly Thélus and
Hill 140 [Hill 135 in text] to the north of the village is vital to the
Third Army operation, in order to deprive the enemy of the observa-
tion into the valleys running south-west from the Vimy ridge.

If it is in any way possible, Thélus and the Hill 140 [Hill 135 in
text] must be captured on the same day as the Third Army operation
takes place.

2.   The enemy has direct observation into the valley north of
Neuville St. Vaast until Hill 145 and La Folie Farm are captured,
and into the valleys south of Neuville St. Vaast and south of Roclincourt until Thélus and Hill 140 [Hill 135 in text] are taken.   It will
be difficult to place field guns sufficiently far forward to cut the wire
of the northern portion of the German intermediate line running
from A.17.d. [Nine Elms] to A.6.a. [Count's Wood] without the
knowledge of the enemy.

The possibility of destroying the wire on this line and of capturing
Thélus on the first day of the operation depends, therefore, on an
adequate supply of the new (106) fuze for the 4·5″ and 6″ Howitzers,
The First Army scheme is drawn up on the assumption that the
supply will be sufficient.

The enemy has good observation up the Carency and Ablain St.
Nazaire valleys from the Pimple and the Bois en Hache.   The
capture of these two points is, therefore, essential to complete the
Vimy Ridge operation.

3.   The front from the Arras—Lens Road to the Lorette Spur
(inclusive) is normally held by rather over 4 German Regiments.
Of these, the equivalent of 4 battalions are in the front line, 4
battalions (or their equivalent) are in support 1,000 to 1,500 yards
in rear, and the remaining 4 battalions are resting some 5 to 6 miles
from the front line.   In addition, two supporting and two resting
battalions of the northern German division to be attacked are available in the neighbourhood of Lens.[1]

---

[1] By April these dispositions had been changed but the alterations
were known (Compiler's Note).

4. It is proposed to divide the First Army operation into two—a Southern attack and a Northern attack.

The Southern attack will be carried out by the Canadian Corps (of 4 Canadian Divisions), with 1 British Division in reserve. The Northern attack will be carried out by troops of the I Corps, on a date subsequent to that on which the Southern attack takes place.

The remainder of the First Army front will be held as follows :—

From the Lorette Spur to a point on the north of the Loos salient by the I Corps, with 3 divisions (less those troops allotted to the Northern attack).

From the left of the I Corps to Picantin by the XI Corps, with 2 divisions.

5. The attack on the blue [subsequently called " red "] objective will be carried out by the leading brigades of the 4 Canadian Divisions, in accordance with the following time-table, which is approximate only :—

Attack on 1st intermediate objective starts at Zero.
Attack on 2nd intermediate objective starts at Zero+20 minutes.
Attack on blue objective starts at Zero $+1\frac{1}{2}$ hours.

The attack on the red [subsequently called Blue and Brown] objective will be carried out by the reserve brigades of the two right divisions, and will take place about five hours after Zero hour.

The scope of the second phase of the operation (red objective) has had to be modified owing to the fact that the enemy are now constructing a new line on the reverse slope of Thélus Hill. His wire already runs from A.6. central [Count's Wood] to B.7. central [Commandant's House]. The attack on this new line, in order to gain the observation over the Douai plain and the Northern attack will be undertaken as separate operations [1] as soon as guns have been moved forward, on Z+2 or Z+3 day. Arrangements for this further operation will be made in consultation with Third Army.

6. It is intended to commence destruction and wire-cutting 3 or 4 weeks before Z day, and to limit the bombardment proper to 48 hours at the outside. There will be no intense bombardment prior to Zero hour. Feint attacks will be carried out at various points on the Army front during the preparation period to make the enemy disclose his guns and barrage lines on the offensive front, and to prevent the movement of reserves from opposite the defensive front.

A few heavy howitzers will be left on the defensive front until the last moment, to assist by registration from several different positions in deceiving the enemy as to the limits of the offensive front.

7. The distribution of artillery on Z day can be summarized briefly as follows :—

(a) Field Guns—18-pdrs.
Per attacking divisions of Canadian Corps .   90 (approx.)
    or 1 per 17 yards of front.

---

[1] Eventually only the Northern attack was a separate operation (Compiler's Note).

24 to 36 guns [subsequently increased to 120] will be dug in,
in forward positions, to support the attack of the Red
[subsequently called Blue and Brown] objective.

For the right division of I Corps   54
    or 1 per 46 yards of front.

(Average) Per Division of I and XI Corps on
               defensive front   45
    or 1 per 170–200 yards of front.

The Field howitzers (less 6 batteries allotted for Counter
Battery work) will be distributed approximately in proportion
to the 18-pdrs.

(*b*) Heavy and Siege guns and howitzers.

On the offensive front will be organized in—

6 (mixed) groups for counter battery work.

10 groups for destruction, which, as they become available, will
gradually reinforce the counter battery groups.

(*c*) On the defensive front there will be—
        4 batteries of 4·7″ or 60-pdrs.
        2 batteries of 6″ howitzers.

8.   It is not proposed to use cylinder gas.

3,000 projectors and 6,000 drums have been asked for for use on
Z day, (*a*) on the left flank of the Southern attack, against Givenchy-
on-Gohelle and the German supporting troops east of the Pimple
and (*b*) against Les Tilleuls and Thélus.

One Special Company (4″ mortars) has been asked for, for use
at selected points against the German troops in the front system in
the mine crater area.

First Army.   H. S. HORNE,
31st January, 1917.   General,
                       Commanding First Army.

BATTLES OF ARRAS

CANADIAN CORPS : SCHEME OF OPERATIONS

FOR BATTLES OF ARRAS

PART I

SECTION I.

GENERAL CONSIDERATIONS :

1. Intention.

The task of the Canadian Corps is to form a strong defensive flank for the operations of the Third Army by the capture of the Vimy Ridge from the Commandant's House to Gunner Crater both inclusive.

The capture of this high ground and especially of Thélus and Hill 140 North of the Village is vital to the Third Army operation in order to deprive the enemy of the observation into the valleys running S.W. from the Vimy Ridge.

2. Importance of Vimy Ridge.

The tactical importance of the Vimy Ridge is increased by the recent developments on the front of the Third and Fifth Armies. As long as he maintains his hold on this Ridge the enemy can withdraw south of Arras even to the Hindenburg Line without compromising the security of his line to the North. He can thus retain possession of the French Manufacturing Districts and the Belgian Coast. The Germans are therefore likely to attach great importance to the Vimy Ridge and to fight hard for its possession. It is already apparent that they have considerably reinforced their line in this Sector.

3. Objectives.

The principal objectives of the Canadian Corps are :—

(i) Thélus and Hill 140 [Hill 135 in text] to the North of it.
(ii) Hill 145 and La Folie Farm.
(iii) The German guns in the Farbus and Goulot Woods.

The importance of (i) has already been stated. As regards (ii) the enemy has direct observation into the valley North of Neuville St. Vaast until Hill 145 and La Folie Farm

are taken. The capture of these features is therefore a
necessary preliminary to that of Hill 140. To effect the
capture of the guns the attack must be pushed through to
the Brown line before nightfall on the first day.

4. Troops Available.

The fighting troops available for the operation are :—

(a) Divisions.

1st, 2nd, 3rd, and 4th Canadian Divisions.
5th (British) Division.

(b) Artillery.

Divisional and Army Brigades.
    5 Divisional Artilleries (10 F.A. Brigades).
    14 Army F.A. Brigades.
    8 additional 18-pounder batteries.
Trench Mortars.
    Medium—From 70 to 96.
    Heavy—20.
Heavy.

Heavy How. Batteries (maximum)			18
Medium ,,	,,	,,	26
4·5″ ,,	,,	,,	3 (attached from Divl. Artillery)
60-pdr. .	.	.	9
6″ Mark VII	.	.	2

(c) Mounted Troops.

Canadian Light Horse (3 Sqdns.).
Canadian Cyclist Battalion (3 Coys.).
1st Canadian Motor Machine Gun Brigade (38 guns).

5. German Forces immediately opposing us.   (Vide Map N)

(a) The German forces opposite the Canadian Corps are :
16th Bavarian Division.
    (14th Bav. R.I.R., 21st Bav. R.I.R., 11th Bav. I.R.)
79th Reserve Division.
    (261st R.I.R., 262nd R.I.R., 263rd R.I.R.)
1st Bavarian Reserve Division.
    (1st or 3rd Bav. R.I.R., 2nd Bavarian R.I.R., 3rd
    or 1st Bav. R.I.R.)
    [The boundaries of the regiments were given.]

(b) Successive Lines of Defence :

The German defences are organized in successive
systems as follows :
    Front Line System, Support Line System, Reserve
    Line System, and Corps Line System.

Front Line System : in each regimental sector is held by
one battalion (4 companies) who are divided between
the firing and immediate support line. In the event
of an attack resistance may be expected in both these
lines. The majority of the Machine guns in this
system are in the Second Line, although the new
08–15 light machine guns will, when received, be
mostly in the firing line.

Support Line System : in each regimental sector is held
by one battalion (4 companies).

It is apparently left to the judgment of the Officer
Commanding a support unit to defend his own line or
to reinforce the front line garrison.

The remaining battalion (4 companies) of each
regiment in the line are at rest billets (coloured
Green) and, in the event of an attack, they would
probably be called upon to man the

Reserve Line System : assisted by the reserve regiments.

Corps Line : is the next defence line, and it would in all
probability be manned by Divisions withdrawn from
rest.

(c) Time required for reinforcements to reach respective
lines of defence.

RESERVE BATTALIONS

Regiment	From Rest at	To Support Line	To Reserve Line
11th Bav. I.R. .	Fosse 2 de Drocourt	13,000 yards 3 hours	11,700 yards 2¾ hours
261st R.I.R. .	Méricourt	9,400 yards 2 hours	7,400 yards 1¾ hours
262nd R.I.R. .	Bois Bernard	10,750 yards 2½ hours	9,500 yards 2 hours
1st or 3rd Bav. R.I.R. . .	Neuvireuil	10,150 yards 2¼ hours	9,650 yards 2 hours
2nd Bav. R.I.R. .	Oppy	9,000 yards 2 hours	7,500 yards 1¾ hours

Reserve Regiments.

263rd R.I.R.	Acheville	7,500 yards	1¾ hrs.
	Rouvroy	8,000 yds.	2 hrs.
	Drocourt	11,200 yds.	2½ hrs.
3rd or 1st Bav. R.I.R.	Willerval	4,000 yds.	1 hr.
	Arleux en Gohelle	6,000 yds.	1¼ hrs.
	Fresnoy	7,600 yds.	1¾ hrs.

(d) Reserves at a distance, but possibly available for this
front :

The 6th Bavarian Reserve Division and the 12th
Reserve Division are both in rest probably in the
neighbourhood of Douai and are both familiar with
this front.   In the event of their being called on
to reinforce, they would probably be brought by
train from Douai to Drocourt or Méricourt.   From
this point they would probably be marched to the
Corps line.

Allowing two hours for entraining at Douai,
travelling and detraining at Méricourt and 1¼ hrs.
for the march, the first troops of the resting
Divisions could reach the Corps line in 3¼ hours

from the time of an alarm. This calculation provides for trains being ready with steam up at Douai.
It is assumed that trains will be ordered as soon as
our final bombardment begins.

SECTION II.

PREPARATORY PHASE.

1. Destruction of Selected Points.
   See Artillery Plan [Appendix 15].

2. Wire Cutting.
   See Artillery Plan [Appendix 15].

3. Harassing Fire by Artillery and Machine Guns.
   It is proposed to continue with nightly tasks for Heavy
and Divisional Artilleries on all Hostile Communications and
approaches within the limits of weekly ammunition allotment.
   This harassing fire will be intensified in accordance with
ammunition available, distinct tasks being allotted to all
Divisional and Heavy Artilleries.
   A map indicating main tracks, communications, approaches, light railways, refilling points, dumps, etc. will
be issued to all concerned to assist in framing night firing
programmes.
   In co-operation with the Artillery, the greatest possible
volume of Machine Gun fire is now being applied, both by
day and night against the following objectives :—
   (i) The targets previously engaged by the Artillery, more
       especially wire entanglements, in order to prevent
       repairs and hinder new work.
   (ii) Communication trenches, roads, tracks, tramways and
        dumps known to be used by the enemy, especially those
        leading to Trench Mortar emplacements.

   As soon as the Divisions occupy their battle fronts and
the density of the M.Gs. permits, it is the intention to engage
by day wire and defences that are not under direct observation and on which the enemy's working parties are probably
active in daylight, and to engage and keep under fire the
hostile batteries located in Bois de la Folie.
   It is contemplated to employ 64 guns by day and 64 guns
by night in harassing fire on the Corps front.

4. Counter Battery Work.
   See Artillery Plan [Appendix 15].

SECTION III.

PLAN OF ATTACK.

1. Successive Stages.
   It is proposed to carry out the operation in four stages,
shown in Map W as the Black, Red, Blue and Brown lines

respectively. In view of the importance of gaining early possession of Hill 140 [Hill 135 in text], the Canadian Corps will push through to the Blue line with as short intermediate pauses as possible.

The XVII Corps has arranged to conform and keep touch with the right of the Canadian Corps up to and including the Blue line. The advance from the Blue to the Brown line will be made to synchronize with that of the XVII Corps.

The advance will be timed as follows :—

Line	Infantry reach (barrage lifts off)	Infantry advance from	Remarks
Black .	Zero plus 35′ (a)	Zero plus 75′	(a) Right of 1st Cdn. Div.
Red .	Zero plus 95′ (a)	Zero plus 245′ (b)	(b) 132′ on right of 1st Cdn. Div.
Blue .	Zero plus 320′	Zero plus 416′ (a)	
Brown	Zero plus 468′		

N.B. These times are subject to slight alteration.

2. Distribution of Troops.

The attack will be carried out by the 4 Divisions of the Canadian Corps advancing at Zero simultaneously with the XVII Corps, the left of which will advance in touch with the right of the Canadian Corps.

The 5th British Division less 1 Inf. Bde. will be in Corps Reserve.

3. Headquarters and Boundaries.

Each Division will assault with two brigades in front and one brigade in reserve. The task of the leading brigades of each Division will be the capture and consolidation of the Red line.

The 1st and 2nd Cdn. Divisions will employ their reserve brigades for the capture and consolidation of the Blue and Brown lines. One Brigade of the 5th (British) Division will be placed at the disposal of the 2nd Canadian Division to assist in the capture of the Blue line.

4. Infantry.

The infantry brigades of each division will be assembled for attack and deployed as follows :—

1st Cdn. Div.   Attacks Black and Red lines with two leading Brigades, each Brigade assaulting with three Battalions, keeping one Battalion in reserve. Attacks Blue and Brown lines with reserve Brigade, which assaults with three Battalions, keeping one Battalion in reserve.

2nd Cdn. Div.   Attacks Black and Red Lines with two leading Brigades, each Brigade assaulting with two Battalions, keeping one Battalion in reserve and 1 Battalion finding " Moppers Up " and carrying parties.

Attacks Blue and Brown lines with two reserve Brigades, (including one Brigade of 5th (British) Division), Right Brigade assaulting with 3 Battalions, keeping one Battalion in reserve ; Left Brigade assaulting with 2 Battalions, keeping one Battalion in reserve, and one Battalion finding " Moppers Up " and carrying parties.

3rd Cdn. Div. Attacks Black and Red Lines with two Brigades, each Brigade assaulting with three Battalions, keeping one Battalion in reserve. One Brigade in reserve.

4th Cdn. Div. Attacks Black and Red lines with two Brigades, each Brigade assaulting with three Battalions, keeping one Battalion in reserve. One Brigade in reserve.

The 5th (British) Division in Corps Reserve, will be assembled by Zero hour as follows :

Div'l H.Q.	. Château d'Acq.
1 Inf. Bde. ⎫ Pioneer Bn. ⎭	Mont St. Eloy.
3 Fd. Coys. R.E.	. Bois des Alleux.
1 Inf. Bde.	. Camblain l'Abbé, Maisnil Bouche.
3 Fd. Ambls.	Cambligneul.

5. Trench Organization.

The construction of jumping-off trenches will be deferred to the last, so as not to attract attention. Except on the front of the 4th Canadian Division, where the German front line is from 250 to 300 yards distant, it will not be necessary to dig advanced trenches, our own front line being cleaned out for the purpose.

In this connection it is to be noted that the enemy's crater posts will give him observation over many of our assembly and jumping-off trenches. It is therefore desirable that Zero should not be later than half-an-hour before sunrise, so that the assembly of assaulting troops may not be detected, but arrangements must be made to allow for a later hour in the event of the latter being decided on.

A considerable number of subways have been constructed to facilitate the passage of troops, the storage of ammunition, water and stores and the forwarding of these through the front system out of reach of shell fire.

The most careful arrangements must be made for the control of traffic in these tunnels, especially with regard to the evacuation of wounded, and included in Divisional Schemes.

6. Method of Advance.

At Zero the shrapnel barrage will begin and the whole of the infantry of the leading Brigades will advance, getting across No Man's Land as soon as possible.

The Reserve Brigades of the 1st and 2nd Canadian Divisions will move forward at such an hour as will enable them to reach and form up behind the Red line in time to advance from it at Zero plus 245′.[1] The advance of these Brigades from their places of assembly will take place at the pre-arranged hour, without further orders, but the pause of $2\frac{1}{2}$ hours on the Red line will allow of their movements being modified in the event of the situation requiring it.

In order to avoid casualties from Artillery fire as few troops as possible will be left in our own front and support lines.

Divisions will be responsible that all preparations are made to facilitate the advance of the infantry through our front system of trenches, by the provision of bridges and ladders and the removal of wire in front and support lines where necessary, due regard being paid to the concealment of this from the enemy until the last moment.

The craters on certain portions of the front, notably that of the 3rd Canadian Division, are a peculiar feature and require special consideration. A careful reconnaissance has been made of these craters, the results of which are embodied in Appendix F.

With a view to making a practical comparison, a selected party of officers visited the crater area at La Boiselle and Fricourt, which is very similar to the one on this front. The general conclusion arrived at is that, with the exception of the big ones of recent formation, such as Montreal and Patricia, the craters do not present an insurmountable obstacle. This opinion is confirmed by the experience of several raids which have been carried out. They must be negotiated by small parties who can take advantage of the causeways formed by the lips, skirting the actual bottoms, which are likely to be wet and holding. The advance of these parties will be covered by a barrage of Stokes Mortars and Rifle Grenades.

Special means of ingress into the Craters will be prepared by a trench or Russian Sap, each individual crater being treated differently.

In the attacks across the La Boiselle and Fricourt fronts the crater groups were avoided and the attacks delivered only over the open ground between the groups. These attacks were subjected to much enfilade fire and it appears that small parties could easily have been pushed through the crater groups to deal with the machine guns posted to enfilade the open spaces and to form a link between the attacks on either side of the groups.

After the Red line has been reached, the 3rd Canadian Division will be responsible for keeping touch with the 2nd Canadian Division in the Bois de Bonval and for protecting the left of the 2nd Canadian Division from any counter-attack coming from the direction of Vimy and the Bois du Goulot.

After the Blue line has been reached, the 3rd Canadian

---

[1] Plus 132′ on right of 1st Cdn. Div.

Division will establish posts at the Northern end of the Bois de Bonval in close touch with the left of the 2nd Canadian Division and will arrange to have one battalion in reserve in the vicinity of Zwischen Stellung in S.29.c. ready for immediate action in the direction indicated.

It is intended that in its advance from the Red line the Left Brigade of the 2nd Canadian Division should turn the North-west end of the Farbus Line, i.e., the new double line of defence running from Commandant's House to Count's Wood, taking it in flank from North-west to South-east.

In the event of any Division or Brigade being held up, the units on the flanks will on no account check their advance, but will form defensive flanks in that direction and press forward themselves so as to envelop the strong point or centre of resistance which is preventing the advance. With this object in view reserves will be pushed in behind those portions of the line that are successful rather than those which are held up.

7. Artillery.

See Artillery Plan [Appendix 15].

8. Machine Guns.

(i) Resources.

The number of machine guns in the five divisions under the Canadian Corps for the purpose of the operations contemplated, is as follows :—

20 M.G. Companies	320 M.G.'s *	(assuming the
1st Cdn. M.M.G. Bde.	38 M.G.'s	5th Division
	——	to have 4 M.G.
* Total	. 358 M.G.'s	Coys.)

(ii) Distribution.

The distribution throughout the various phases of the operation will be as follows :—

With the assaulting brigades for consolidation	130 M.G.'s
Barrages and supporting fire	150 M.G.'s
In reserve & reorganizing	78 M.G.'s [1]
	——
Total	358 M.G.'s

(iii) Organization.

For the sake of simplicity, the guns detailed for supporting and barrage fire will be organized into batteries and groups of batteries. The batteries will be composed of 8 guns, and a group will be made of two or more batteries. There will be a group for every Brigade front, and the number of Machine Guns for supporting and barrage fire will approximate one for every 50 yards of front. The batteries will invariably be designated by the letter of their respective barrage.

[1] This number may be reduced by 16 if the 4th Machine Gun Company of the 5th Division does not arrive in time.

(iv) Dispositions.

Protective barrages will be established at each definite stage of the operations. Owing to the distance to which it is intended to penetrate the German lines on the 1st and 2nd Canadian Divisional fronts, it will be necessary to move machine gun batteries forward immediately after the capture of the Red objective, and later after the capture of the Blue line.

The Machine Gun Batteries of the Black line will move forward to their assigned Blue line positions under the covering fire of the Machine Gun batteries of the Red line, reaching their positions in time to support the attack of the Blue line.

After the capture of the Blue line, the move of the Machine Gun Batteries forward to their assigned Brown line positions will be made in echelon, one battery at a time. As a precautionary measure, the Machine Gun Batteries of the Red line in 1st and 2nd Canadian Divisional areas will remain in position until the Brown line is taken, and permission to withdraw has been received from Corps Headquarters.

The protective and final barrages, and the corresponding disposition of the guns, are shown on a tracing [omitted].

Supporting fire will be available practically at every stage of the advance.

(v) Control.

The machine gun barrages and fire organizations are co-ordinated by the Corps Machine Gun Officer, and no alterations are to be made without reference to Corps Headquarters.

The Divisions will retain control of the guns covering their own Sectors and may from time to time allot special secondary targets to any group of guns without prejudice to the final barrage, which must remain the primary consideration.

The Brigades will be given a call on the guns covering their Sector, and fire may be applied or withheld at the request of the Brigade Commander.

(vi) Liaison.

To facilitate the forward liaison, the Group Commanders will be personally at Battle Headquarters of their affiliated Brigades, or at the Headquarters of a Battalion of the Brigade, as may be more convenient. They will be connected with their Batteries by buried cable in the first phase, and in the subsequent phases by visual flare signals and runners. Telephones will be established as soon as possible.

Liaison with the Divisions will be maintained through Brigade Headquarters.

Liaison between Divisional Headquarters and Corps will be by telephone (Special line to Corps M.G. Officer).

(vii) <u>Supply of Ammunition, Water & Oil.</u>

Ammunition supply has been calculated on the basis of 15,000 rounds per gun per day for a period of three days.

Cooling water will be provided in petrol tins at the rate of 4 gallons per gun per day.

The supply of lubricating oil will be calculated on the basis of $\frac{1}{4}$ pint per gun per day.

(viii) <u>Distribution of Personnel.</u>

For the purpose of reducing the casualties in trained personnel, the following distribution has been adopted :—

For each Section of 4 guns :

" A "	At the guns	. . .	1 Officer.
			1 Sergeant.
			1 Corporal.
			16 Men.
" B "	With the M.G. Coy. Comdr.	.	4 Men.
" C "	At a convenient place in vicinity of Divnl. H.Q.	. . .	4 Men.
" D "	At transport lines	. .	1 Officer.
			1 Sergeant.
			1 Corporal.
			6 Men.

NOTE.—B will be used to replace casualties immediately.

C will not be used without reference to the G.O.C. affiliated Brigades or Div. H.Q.

D will not be used until the Company is withdrawn from the line.

In addition, two infantry men will be attached to each gun as ammunition carriers, total of 32 men per Company. The Infantry Brigades will be responsible for replacing casualties to ammunition carriers.

One trained gunner and two infantry ammunition carriers per gun will be equipped with tump lines or some other form of equipment for carrying ammunition.

(ix) <u>Pack Transport.</u>

All available pack animals with the four Machine Gun Companies in each Division will be grouped into Divisional Pack Trains and will be used under the Divisional Machine Gun Officer to keep the Machine Guns supplied with ammunition, water, oil and rations.

(x) <u>Repair Shop.</u>

A small repair shop will be established well forward in each Division to effect all possible immediate repairs to Machine Guns.

9. <u>Mounted Troops.</u>

1 Squadron Canadian Light Horse,
1 Company Canadian Cyclists Battalion,
will be in Corps Reserve and assembled, ready for immediate action, in the vicinity of Bois des Alleux by Zero plus 2 hours.

The remainder of the Cavalry and Cyclists will be employed as follows :—

1 Troop Canadian Light Horse 1 Platoon Cyclists	With each Division for escort and despatch rider duty.
1 Troop Canadian Light Horse 1 Platoon Cyclists	Under A.P.M. Canadian Corps for escort duty and traffic control.
120 Dismounted Cavalry and Cyclists.	Attached to 1st Cdn. Motor M.G. Bde. for carrying, etc.

The 1st Canadian Motor Machine Gun Brigade will be employed for covering and barrage fire as shown in Section 8 (1).

10. Tanks.

One Company (i.e., 8) Tanks are expected to be available, and will be placed at the disposal of the 2nd Canadian Division for use as follows :—

(i) Four Tanks will assist in the capture of Thélus by working along the perimeter trenches N. and S. of the Village.

(ii) Four Tanks will assist in the capture of Thélus and Farbus Lines, working down the Farbus Line from Count's Wood towards the Heroes' Wood. Detailed plans are being worked out and will be submitted by the 2nd Canadian Division.

In any case it is essential that the Infantry plan and the Artillery barrage should be quite independent of the action of Tanks, so that in the event of the latter breaking down the arrangements are not upset.

11. Aircraft.

(i) Aeroplanes : No. 16 Squadron will furnish contact patrols to fly at specified hours, which will be communicated later. Every man of assaulting troops will carry two flares for communication with aircraft.

Messages will be dropped at Advanced Divisional Headquarters and a landing place has been prepared West of Château de la Haie to facilitate communication with Advanced Corps Headquarters at Camblain l'Abbé.

(ii) Kite Balloons : [1] It is suggested that for purposes of deception as large a concentration of Kite Balloons as possible should be effected about Zero minus 10 or 12 days, in the neighbourhood of the Aubers Ridge or Messines. This concentration should be combined with a carefully executed system of registration by a few heavy howitzers and guns. The effect would be considerably enhanced if a consistent scheme of leakage was organized on the telephones in the forward area throughout the First and Second Armies, all messages tending towards the same conclusion, i.e. an offensive against the Aubers or Messines Ridge. A suitable display of tents in the area would also be useful.

[1] It is understood that this proposal has been adopted.

12. Gas and Smoke.

It is understood that the following resources will be available for the Canadian Corps :—

Special Bde. R.E.   .   1 Special Coy. (For Mortars).
                         3 Coys. of a Special Battalion
                         (For cylinders and Projectors).
Resources   .   .   Gas Projectors—2,000.
                         Drums   —4,000.
                         Cylinders   —as required.

It is intended to devote the bulk of the projectors and drums to dealing with the Pimple (S.9.a.) in conjunction with the smoke from the T.M.'s in order to neutralize the observation from this point at Zero.

The 4″ Stokes Mortars will be mainly employed, in conjunction with 18-pdr. and 4·5″ Smoke Shell, to smoke Hill 145 and La Folie Crest at Zero, also Hill 140 [Hill 135 in text] if the wind serves. It is also proposed to employ them with " Thermit " to barrage the trenches immediately in rear of the Craters on the front of the 3rd Canadian Division, which cannot be effectively dealt with by 18-pdr. A reconnaissance for this purpose is being made.

It was the intention to discharge cylinder gas during the later stages of the preparatory phase. In the light of recent experience, however, it is considered that in view of the uncertainty of its action, the installation of cylinders is not worth the immense labour involved.

13. Mining.

1. Mines have been prepared and placed for the following purposes :—
(a) To destroy enemy crater posts.
(b) To defilade suspected strong positions.
(c) To destroy portions of the enemy front line trenches.
(d) To open up Communication Trenches by bored mines.
(e) To create diversions.
2. Infantry Subways have been constructed to facilitate the rapid passage of the Infantry through the trench-mortared area. These are being further developed and dug-out accommodation for Brigade and Battalion Headquarters, Heavy T.M. Emplacements, Ammunition and Bomb Stores, Dressing Stations, etc., in accordance with the requirements of Divisions, are being provided as time, labour and materials permit.
3. The scheme is shown upon the attached map " S ", and details are given in the attached Appendix " G ".
4. Excellent progress has been made by all the R.E. Tunnelling Companies, and all the proposals will be completed by March 15th, with the following exceptions—
(a) The offensive mine against the Pimple cannot be completed before April 15th.
(b) The extension of Tottenham Subway under Zouave Valley cannot be completed before April 1st.
(c) Only one half of the T.M. Emplacements in Grange and Goodman Subways can be completed by March 15th.

D

(*d*) The connection between Pylones and Goodman Subways cannot be completed until about April 1st.

(*e*) The connection through Zivy Subway, the mine system and by the Russian Sap to the Phillips Group for cable cannot be completed until about April 1st.

SECTION IV.

CONSOLIDATION.

The Red Line will be consolidated by the two leading Brigades of each Division.

The Blue and Brown Lines will be consolidated by the Reserve Brigades of the 1st and 2nd Canadian Divisions.

The system of consolidation after the final objective has been reached will be as follows :—

(*a*) An Outpost Line of detached Lewis Gun Posts approximately along the line of German Gun Positions in Farbus and Goulot Woods, continued inside the Western edge of the Bois de la Folie. This line will eventually become the front line.

(*b*) An observation line in front (i.e. East) of the crest of the Ridge (Commandant's House—Thélus Mill—Hill 145) covering all necessary O.P.'s. This Line will eventually become the support line.

(*c*) A Main Resistance line behind the crest of the Ridge. This line will form the Reserve Line and will be provided with as many deep dug-outs as possible, old German ones being made full use of. These dug-outs will hold the reserves on whose offensive action the defence of the Ridge will mainly depend.

Detailed schemes of consolidation in accordance with these principles are being worked out by Divisions and included in the practice trenches over which the troops are trained. Map O shows the general scheme.

As the configuration of the ground will probably give very little field of fire to the front from (*b*), the defence of this line and of (*c*) must chiefly depend on the enfilading fire of well-sited machine guns. Arrangements for the organization of these are being worked out in detail. The actual siting of lines (*b*) and (*c*) must be done on the ground by Divisional and Brigade Staffs. The map does not give sufficient indication for this to be satisfactorily done beforehand.

When operations begin and the mines have been fired, the 182nd, 185th, 172nd and a portion of the 176th Tunnelling Companies R.E. will be freed to assist in the provision of well-protected dug-out accommodation in the new position by reclaiming old and damaged German dug-outs, making necessary alterations to them, and by the construction of new tunnelled dug-outs.

Should circumstances permit, it is anticipated that approximately one Tunnelling Company R.E. will be available to assist each Division in the provision of the necessary accommodation. It is proposed, as far as the supply of materials will permit, to have a supply of mining sets and lagging prepared and kept in reserve for this purpose.

Where conditions are considered favourable, time and labour may be saved by blowing communication trenches from bored mines.

SECTION V.

COMMUNICATIONS.

1. Buried Cable.

(a) Initial System.

An extensive system of deeply buried cable is being installed along the whole Corps front, involving the employment of from 500 to 700 men per night, for the last two months. This system, which is nearly completed, is shown in Map Q. The allotment of pairs has been provisionally made and provides fully for Infantry Brigades to Divisions, Artillery Groups to Batteries, and Batteries to O.P.'s.

(b) Forward extension after capture of objective.

It is intended to push forward buried lines on the first night if possible, in order to secure safe communication with the new O.P.'s on the Ridge. These extensions are also shown on Map Q. In principle, each Division will concentrate on getting one forward line through to the most important point. Subways are being employed to the fullest extent to carry the cable forward. The Canadian Corps Signal Company will provide a Cable Section for each Division to supervise the laying of the cable.

2. Airline.

Airline trestle routes have been pushed forward to within 2,000 yards of the present front line.

A dump of stores for airline and buried cable construction is being made at La Targette.

3. Wireless and Power Buzzers.

(a) Wireless.

It is proposed to put one trench set at each of the Brigades in the line, each set having three operators. These sets will work back to two forward directing stations, which will be in touch with Divisional Headquarters and a central control station at Mont St. Eloy, which will be in touch with the Corps Signals Exchange there (Gerrard).

(b) Buzzer.

Each Brigade in the line to have one Amplifier manned by Wireless Personnel and two Power Buzzers. One Power Buzzer will go forward on each Brigade frontage with Infantry, and will be operated by a party of 2 Battalion signallers specially trained for the work. A third trained signaller will remain at Brigade Headquarters with the spare Buzzer to go forward if necessary.

Detail of Work.

The Amplifier, if possible, to be in a mine gallery and connected by a buried cable route to Brigade Headquarters or after Brigades have advanced to the Divisional report centre.

The Buzzer will keep repeating its message till told to stop by a rocket fired from its own Amplifier.

(c) Codes and Cipher.

The question of a code and calls for stations is being considered and will be made as simple as possible. (To be communicated later.)

4. Pigeons.

The Pigeon Service has been arranged as follows :

Position of Lofts : There are 4 Lofts, one for each Division :

1st Cdn. Div. to use Ecoivres Mobile Loft—No. 11.
2nd Cdn. Div. to use Mont St. Eloy Mobile Loft—No. 2.
3rd Cdn. Div. to use Camblain l'Abbé Mobile Loft—No. 9.
4th Cdn. Div. to use Stationary Loft—Sains en Gohelle.

Each of the above lofts is well placed and near to telephonic communication except for 4th Canadian Division which is too far North though in close touch with Signals.

Two more mobile lofts are on their way from Boulogne and may be in time for use, which will enable 4th Canadian Division to have a loft at Château de la Haie.

Forward Cage. A forward cage will be established at 2nd Canadian Division Report Centre at Aux Rietz. Here a reserve of 20 birds will be held and three runners as carriers.

Allotment of Birds. The allotment of 6 Birds per Brigade in the line will be delivered to above cage every day from the various lofts by motor cyclist. Battalion Orderlies, working under orders of Brigade Signals, will carry birds from cage to trench stations of all four Divisions.

Battalion Orderlies. Each Battalion now has its establishment of six pigeon orderlies.

Extra Birds. In the event of two new Mobile Lofts arriving in time, the above allotment might be increased very slightly, but otherwise it will be only able to increase the number for special days.

5. Visual.

A system of visual communication is being worked out by each Division for its own area.

SECTION VI.

MAPS.

1.   In addition to the lithographed maps issued by First Army (scales 1/10,000 and 1/20,000) special maps (scale 1/5,000) are in preparation. These were laid down with reference to battle fronts and objectives of the four Divisions of the Corps, and will be issued on a scale sufficient to place them in the hands of all officers and Senior N.C.O.'s of Infantry Battalions. A limited number of sheets of adjoining Divisions will be issued to each Division.

2.   Maps are being printed on Zigad paper (scale 1/10,000) for use with brief size Ellam's Duplicator, on which is shown only the topography and grid.

These also were laid down with reference to battle fronts and objectives of the four Divisions of the Corps, and it is proposed to issue these from day to day as the action progresses with all available information added by use of the Ellam's Duplicator.

3.   Maps are now in stock (and more on order) on Zigad paper, scale 1/20,000, for use with brief size Ellam's Duplicator, upon which are shown our own and the enemy's trenches.   It is proposed to issue these to Divisions as required, adding additional information by means of Ellam's Duplicator.

4.   A visibility map (Map P attached), scale 1/10,000, has been prepared and issued to all concerned, showing by means of references in different colours and designs the portion of the enemy country which can be seen from various Artillery O.P.'s.   It is thought that this would be of great assistance to new batteries arriving on the front.

5.   It is proposed to publish, if time be available, a limited edition of 1/20,000 upon which will be shown all known information of enemy's tramways, roads, tracks, hutments, headquarters, field kitchens, divisional and regimental sectors, etc.

This map will be issued down to Artillery Brigades.

SECTION VII.

PRISONERS OF WAR.

1. System of Evacuation.

Divisional Collecting Stations

to

Corps Cage

to

Staging Point.

Coupigny Prisoners of War Camp

to

Railhead.   (Chocques.)

2. Arrangements for Examination.

Divisional Collecting Stations :

Preliminary examination by Intelligence Officers during first hours of attack.

Corps Cage.

Interrogation and examination of documents—
4 Intelligence Officers (3 to be lent by Army).
2 Intelligence police.
Interpreters from " IT " personnel.

Advanced Corps H.Q.

Collation and transmission of information—
1 Intelligence Officer.

Army H.Q.

Further examination of selected prisoners by Army Intelligence Officers.

SECTION VIII.

MISCELLANEOUS.

1. Distinguishing Flags.

The following flags will be carried on a scale of 2 per Platoon :—

1st Cdn. Div.	Dark Blue and Yellow.
2nd Cdn. Div.	Yellow Flag with Black Maple Leaf. Reverse side Khaki.
3rd Cdn. Div.	Black and Red.
4th Cdn. Div.	Red.

Strict orders will be given that flags are to be carried in the hand and not stuck into the ground, in order to avoid mistakes which might be caused by flags left behind in evacuated positions.

NOTE.—This document is undated. It was evidently issued with a covering letter bearing a date, but the latter is not in the records.

LETTER FROM LIEUT.-GENERAL SIR L. E. KIGGELL, C.G.S., TO MAJOR-GENERAL N. MALCOLM, M.G.G.S. FIFTH ARMY, 5TH FEBRUARY 1917

Dear Malcolm,

With reference to the plan of the Fifth Army operations, dated the 30th January, the Commander-in-Chief does not like the statement that the objective of the Fifth Army is Achiet-le-Grand. He points out that the rôle of the Fifth Army is to strike the enemy as strong and vigorous a blow as possible on the front between Gueudecourt and Beaumont Hamel and to follow this up in the general direction of Achiet-le-Grand as rapidly as possible with the objects of breaking the enemy's front and attracting as many of his reserves as possible in order to facilitate the operations of the Third Army, with which the Fifth Army should aim at joining hands in the direction of St. Leger so as to envelop the bulk of the hostile troops in the Gommecourt salient.

The Commander-in-Chief recognizes that, with the forces at your disposal, it will probably be necessary to operate in " bites ", and that, of course, the extent of each " bite " must depend on the number of divisions and guns allotted to the Fifth Army.

The dates given in your scheme will very probably prove to be too late and you should be prepared to make your final advance by the 15th March, i.e., to make your preparations on the probability that the Third Army operations will commence shortly after the 15th March.

I will write officially on the subject in a day or two, but meanwhile I send you this warning so that the Army commander and yourself can be working out the amendments in your programme which seem likely to be necessary . . .

The Commander-in-Chief thinks that the accession of the Anzac Corps to the Fifth Army command may enable you to undertake more than is contemplated in the plan sent in. He wants this considered and reported on. And he wishes the preliminary operations to be based on the general idea of enabling you to launch as formidable a blow as possible shortly before the Third Army opens its attack.

Yours very sincerely,
L. E. KIGGELL.

BATTLES OF ARRAS
THIRD ARMY APPRECIATION, No. G.S. 1/15, 7TH FEBRUARY 1917

The object of the operations is to pierce the lines of the German defences between Feuchy Chapel and the Scarpe, that is on a front of 4,000 yards, and then to advance southward, at the same time widening the gap through which the first advance has been made.[1]

The operations are dealt with as follows :—

1. The preliminary concentration.
2. The artillery preparation.
3. The assault of the various lines of defence.
4. The advance of the infantry beyond those lines.
5. The advance of the cavalry.
6. The advance southward.
7. The withdrawal of worn out divisions.
8. The consolidation of our flanks and rear.
9. Further possibilities.[2]

1.   At an early date each of the three attacking corps, VII, VI and XVII, will be made up to three divisions, and the fourth division for each of these corps will shortly be allotted. Each corps will probably place a portion of its three attacking divisions in the front line.

It is important that the concentration of these divisions should not be known to the enemy. Care is to be taken to remove all identity marks from raiding parties and from troops of the front line which are in positions likely to be raided ; all troops should also be specially warned that if captured they must not tell to what division they belong or what troops are near them.

As time goes on a greater concentration will become necessary in the forward areas both of troops and guns in order to clear back areas for reserves. Every means must be taken to conceal

---

[1] Although this appreciation was written before the German retreat to the Hindenburg Line and further modified by the Commander-in-Chief's refusal to allow the attack to be launched after a hurricane bombardment of only two days, it is printed because it is the only single document embodying the ideas of the commander of the Third Army and the methods of the attack. (Compiler's note.)

[2] Para. 10 was a subsequent addition. (Compiler's note.)

the presence of a greater number of troops and guns from aircraft, and no increase in the usual expenditure of ammunition on the front of the Army must be permitted.

The concealment of the increase of horses and transport vehicles is of importance, and standings must be chosen with this end in view. All standings must be clear of the roads in order that the full width of the roads may be used for movement.

Traffic circuits now in use, and others likely to be used, must be carefully inspected, and narrow places and difficult turnings must be improved.

Orders must be issued to ensure that traffic control police are obeyed, and staff and other officers must make it their duty to clear blocks in traffic.

After each corps is brought up to four divisions, five more divisions arrive and will eventually be accommodated east of the Doullens—St. Pol road ; and on the day previous to the attack, three divisions of cavalry will be brought into the area. The situation of troops will then be as shown on map P. 1.

At this stage and before it, horses now under cover must be put in the open and stables are to be converted for the accommodation of men. Plans for the preparation of stables for the use of troops are to be prepared.

On the arrival of the five divisions in Army reserve, one of them will come under the command of the Cavalry Corps, and the remainder under the command of the XVIII Corps. The XVIII Corps will prepare a suitable headquarters for the further operations. The one division which will hold the defensive flank will come under the command of the XIX Corps. The XIX Corps, in addition to administering this division, will surpervise the training of the drafts at the three corps training centres, and, as divisions are withdrawn from the attack, they will be trained and administered by the XIX Corps.

Eventually, when some of these divisions have recovered, it is probable that the XIX Corps will be used in order to maintain the offensive.

2. The artillery preparation for the assault will be of 48 hours' duration. During this period the fire will be continuous and of equal cadence.

The object of this comparatively short bombardment is to obtain the advantage of surprise, and as the rate of fire is not to be increased previous to the assault it is expected that the assault itself will be a surprise.

One third of the total number of guns and howitzers will be rested in turn.

The artillery personnel will be so arranged that every officer and man rests during 12 hours in 24.

For the destruction of the trenches and wire of the first line system, trench mortars will be chiefly employed. Arrangements are to be made to ensure that the personnel of trench-mortar batteries obtain sufficient rest.

The object of these instructions is that the artillery should be fresh and in full strength when the assault begins.

The infantry advancing under the barrage is likely to meet physical obstacles while traversing the first line system ; the rate of advance of the barrage therefore, up to the Black line, should be about 100 yards in six minutes. When more open ground is gained such as exists between the systems of defence, the rate of advance of the barrage should be 100 yards in 4 minutes.

It is to be remembered that the barrage cannot be called back to the infantry, and it is safer for the infantry to wait for the barrage to advance than for the barrage to outstrip the progress of the infantry.

On the advance of the infantry the German guns will be dealt with by the heavier natures of howitzers and guns.

3.   The first assault on the German front line system should be made at an hour which will admit of the troops having a satisfactory breakfast in daylight before attacking—care is to be taken that this meal is a good one.

Each of the nine assaulting divisions will probably have three brigades in the front line.

This will admit of sufficient troops being available to deal with German strong points and the garrisons of dug-outs so as to enable the leading waves to move direct to their objectives.

It is estimated that the Black line will be reached in about one hour.

On this line a halt of one hour will be made in order to pass through the troops who will attack the positions marked by the Blue line.

Starting then from the Black line at Z+2 hours, the Blue line should be reached in 40 minutes.

After gaining this line a halt of 4 hours will be necessary in order to bring up troops for the attack of the Brown line, and in order to bring forward artillery to selected positions in advance of their original positions.

The advance from the Blue line, which should begin at Z+6 hours 40 minutes, will begin to assume the nature of open warfare—generally speaking, a distance of 2,500 yards separates the Blue line from the Brown line, and between these lines there are few lines of defence or strong points, except in front of the VII Corps.

During this advance the whole of the German artillery should be overrun, if it has not been taken away previous to our advance.

In this connection it is important that the troops, while in occupation of the Blue line, should reach points from which the whole of the ground up to the Brown line can be observed ; and rifle and machine-gun fire on the German emplacements must be continuous.

The resting battalions of the German divisions in the front line may be expected to be advancing to counter-attack during this period—it is of importance that their movements should be prevented and that they be overwhelmed by fire.

It is estimated that the advance from the Blue to the Brown line will occupy a period of about two hours.

Consequently our artillery will be concentrated on the Brown line for a period of 6 hours, that is, from the capture of the Blue line at Z+2 hours 40 minutes to the arrival of our infantry on the Brown line at Z+8 hours 40 minutes.

This is a short bombardment for a defensive line of this nature. It is estimated however that, as the resting battalions of the German divisions of the front line will already have been involved in the fight, and further reserves will not yet have come up, the Brown line will be weakly held.

The wire in front of it is not likely to be thoroughly cut owing to the length of range from the original positions of our heavy howitzers. It is therefore important to ensure that all troops possess wire-breakers and wire-cutters and that they are trained in using them.

At this period, the beginning of open warfare, it must be realized that the maintenance of the forward movement depends on the determination and power of direction of the commanders of sections, platoons, companies and battalions. The habit of digging a trench and getting into it, or of waiting for scientifically arranged artillery barrage before advancing, must be discarded.

A slow advance will give time for German reinforcements to arrive. If the advance is continued with reasonable rapidity it is probable that the resistance will quickly lessen, and that we shall reach places in which there are no German troops other than those running away in front of us.

The rapidity of our advance should enable us to capture all the German artillery on the ground over which we move—other German batteries outside this zone will be dealt with by our guns, and it will take a long time before the Germans can concentrate any artillery in front of us.

A few " sticky " company commanders may not only delay the whole operation, but will also be the cause of unnecessary casualties—this must be clearly understood by all.

Artillery as well as infantry must shake off the habits of trench warfare. Battery commanders must be prepared to use their initiative and be able to make rapid reconnaissance followed by rapid movement. Any fear of damage to horses and guns in endeavours to support the infantry at close ranges must not be considered, and direct fire will become common.

4.   It is considered probable that, owing to the disorganization caused by our rapid advance, it will be possible to continue the movement of the VII Corps to the line of the Cojeul river, and that of the VI Corps to the Monchy-le-Preux high ground, either by using the remainder of the three assaulting divisions or by employing the reserve divisions of these corps.

In this case Monchy-le-Preux should be in our hands by nightfall on the first day.

Whatever the positions gained by nightfall, it is important that during the hours of darkness strong outposts should be pushed well in advance of the general front line in order that the Germans may be prevented from reorganizing and digging new lines. A wide belt of neutral ground in front of our line must be maintained in order to give space for the advance of our cavalry at dawn on the second day : for this purpose posts should be established on all points of tactical importance for one or two miles in front of our general line. The corps mounted troops should be used for this purpose as well as infantry. It is therefore necessary to decide on the preliminary distribution of corps mounted troops. Companies and squadrons so detached need have no fear of capture if they act boldly, as the situation will be obscure to the Germans.

From the afternoon or evening of the first day until about midnight, the roads in Arras and east and west of the town must be kept clear for the movement of artillery.

5.   At about midnight the two leading cavalry divisions will begin their march through Arras.   Each division is nine miles long and is estimated to march at 3 miles an hour.   The northern division will march by the main St. Pol—Arras road and the main Arras—Cambrai road and it will probably debouch about Monchy-le-Preux at dawn on the second day.

The southern division will, simultaneously with the northern division, enter Arras by the Faubourg d'Amiens, and, moving through the town on to the Arras—Neuville Vitasse road and then via Tilloy-les-Mofflaines, will debouch at dawn, in line with the northern cavalry division.

Following these two cavalry divisions, a third cavalry division will move down the Crinchon valley through Wailly and Agny, and follow in reserve.

Meanwhile the infantry division allotted to the Cavalry Corps, moving by brigades, will follow the two leading cavalry divisions, two brigades will march by the main St. Pol—Arras road and the third by the Faubourg d'Amiens.

The first objective of the Cavalry Corps will be the line of the Cojeul river between Wancourt and Etaing—a front of 6½ miles.

The second objective will be the line of the Sensée river between Croisilles and Etaing—a front of 7 miles.

The third objective will be the front Croisilles, Ecoust St. Mein, Quéant, Buissy, Ecourt St. Quentin, a front of 12 miles, at which time the cavalry will be supported by the infantry division attached to the Cavalry Corps and by the advance of the XVIII Corps.

With the cavalry, as with the infantry, the essence of success lies in moving forward rapidly before German reinforcements arrive on the scene.   Once the ground is gained it will not be difficult to hold it against counter-attacks, having in view the great increase of fire power now made available by machine guns.

As soon as the cavalry begins to advance, two field artillery brigades from the XVII Corps will be attached to the Cavalry Corps.

During the cavalry advance, patrols must be pushed out to capture the headquarters of German divisions which are within reach, and to destroy telegraphs and railways.

German reinforcements may be expected from the direction of Douai and from Cambrai.   Those coming from Douai will have to negotiate the river crossings and swamps about Arleux. Those from Cambrai should be checked on the crossings of the Canal du Nord.

If reinforcements are required by the Cavalry Corps the VI Corps must be called upon, in order to leave the XVIII Corps complete for its operations in a southerly direction.

6.   The XVIII Corps begins its advance through Arras as soon as the infantry division attached to the Cavalry Corps is clear.

This hour is estimated at Z+24, or the morning of the second day.

It will move on two roads. The northern two divisions will march by the St. Pol—Arras road and through the Baudimont Gate, thence by the main Arras—Cambrai road, moving on this road till they deploy southward, with their left on Chérisy.

The two southern divisions will enter Arras by the Faubourg d'Amiens and move out by the Neuville-Vitasse road, then by Tilloy-les-Mofflaines on Wancourt. On reaching about Wancourt they will deploy southwards, with their right about Héninel.

It is estimated that the leading troops will reach their places of deployment about noon on the second day and that the whole of the four divisions will be concentrated by about 9 P.M. This calculation is based on a division, less artillery, field ambulances, train, etc. being nine miles long, and on the rate of marching being 2 miles an hour.

Divisional artilleries and other batteries will come under the command of the XVIII Corps as it passes through Arras.

In order to carry out the movement of the XVIII Corps, march discipline is necessary. Detailed instructions are required with regard to the amount of transport taken, the equipment and supplies which the troops are to carry, and everything that will tend to the fighting efficiency of these divisions after a slow and difficult march, beginning very early on the second day and ending about 9 P.M. that night—It is hoped that the troops will be able to rest from 9 P.M. till dawn on the third day.

In this case the change from trench to open warfare will have its effect as far up as the corps staff. Dug-out headquarters and cable communications will cease to exist. Staffs will move with the troops, and staff and other officers will require horses. The employment of the corps mounted troops requires consideration.

On the morning of the third day the cavalry and advanced infantry will be fighting on the front indicated above. It is at this period that the XVIII Corps will advance to make good first, the line St. Leger, Ecoust, Quéant, and then Mory, Vaulz Vraucourt, Morchies, Quéant, with a view to preventing movement on the Bapaume—Cambrai road, and on the railway to the south of it.

7.   It is to be noted that when the line Croisilles, Quéant is reached, the total perimeter occupied by the Third Army is 30 miles, and if the line Mory, Vaulz Vraucourt, Morchies, Quéant is gained, this perimeter will increase to 37 miles.

It will therefore be necessary, as soon as troops reach the places allotted to them on the northern, eastern and western portions of this perimeter, for entrenchments and obstacles to be prepared quickly.

It is however considered impossible to bring forward any supplies of R.E. material for some time after the troops reach these places. Every use must be made of everything that is found on the ground.

8.   In this position, the Third Army will have used up its offensive resources until broken divisions can be replaced by fresh reserves. A battle will be in progress on the whole of this perimeter. Our

only way to reduce its length is to push southwards from the line Chat Maigre, Mercatel, Hénin-sur-Cojeul.

Our main object at this period will be to press on the rear of the German divisions holding their original front between Gomme-court and Ficheux, while holding off attacks that will be made on us from the north, east and south.

Such a battle will continue until the Fifth Army can join hands with the Third Army between Achiet-le-Grand and Mory.

If this junction is effected and the positions are held, it should be a matter of a few days before the encircled German divisions are compelled to surrender owing to lack of ammunition and food.

9.   It will be noticed that from Zero till Z + 48 the two main roads leading into Arras will be filled by a stream of troops moving forward. Nothing must check this stream. Roads N. of the Scarpe are allotted to and controlled by the XVII Corps.

The road from Blangy, running south-east to the main Arras —Cambrai road is in bad repair and is not likely to be fit for traffic for several days.

The road through Baudimont Gate and the road through the Faubourg d'Amiens are both capable of carrying three lines of traffic. It may therefore be safe to allow motor ambulance columns to return by these roads, but until the troops are clear it will not be possible to allow motor traffic in both directions.

It must therefore be clearly understood that between Z and Z + 48 hours :—

    i. No replenishment of ammunition can take place.
    ii. No supplies can be sent forward.
    iii. Only a limited number of wounded can be evacuated.
    iv. Prisoners cannot be brought back further than Arras.
    v. Worn out divisions must remain on the ground they have won.

These points apply chiefly to the VI, VII, and XVIII Corps. The XVII Corps, north of the Scarpe, will be able to make their own arrangements, providing the main Arras—St. Pol road is not touched.

With regard to the above, arrangements must be made for all troops and horses to carry three days' rations in addition to the iron ration. This cannot be done if the great-coat and water-proof sheet are also carried.

Definite orders as to dress and equipment must therefore be issued, bearing in mind the various tasks allotted to divisions.

Ammunition sufficient for the period mentioned must be deposited in or in front of Arras, as well as supplies and all engineering materials.

10.   Alternative roads :
Should the two main roads through Arras become impassable, columns will be diverted on alternative routes as follows :—

    (a) South of Arras.
        (i) Northern column via Agnez-les-Duisans and Warlus or via Wagnonlieu, thence through Achicourt and Beaurains to Tilloy-les-Mofflaines, and the Arras—

Cambrai main road.   Or from Achicourt, via Ronville and St Sauveur.

(ii) Southern column, Bac du Sud, Bailleulval, Grosville, Agny, B.M.91.371, Beaurains, Tilloy-les-Mofflaines.

(b) North of Arras.

    (i) Northern column, Louez, St. Aubin, Anzin, St. Nicholas, St. Laurent Blangy, Athies, and south over the Scarpe river.

    (ii) Southern column.   Bernaville, Warlus, Duisans, French military road south of the Scarpe to Blangy and thence to main Arras—Cambrai road.

L. J. BOLS, Major-General,
General Staff, Third Army.

7th February 1917.

BATTLES OF ARRAS

FIRST ARMY ARTILLERY PLAN FOR THE CAPTURE OF VIMY RIDGE, 8TH FEBRUARY 1917

1-4.   ....

5.   The heavy artillery will be divided into 3 C.B. Groups and 8 Siege Groups for trench destruction in the case of the Canadian Corps, and into 3 C.B. Groups and 2 Siege Groups in the I Corps.

6.   To assist the B.G., H.A. Canadian Corps to deal with the large number of Siege Groups (8), and to simplify the work as regards communications and the O.Ps., as well as to form as close liaison as possible between the Heavy Artillery, engaged in trench destructions, and the Infantry, a group Commander may be placed in command of two or more groups, allotted to the destructive work in the zone over which a Division will attack.   The Commander will then be responsible for the following :—

   (a) He should live in the closest touch with the Divisional Commander on whose front he is working, ensuring that his wishes with regard to the work of destruction on his front are passed on to the B.G., H.A. and dealt with to his satisfaction.

   (b) He should receive the orders of the B.G., H.A. of the Corps of his Command, and issue them to his Groups and batteries, working out the details as to allotment of tasks.

   (c) He would be responsible for the liaison work between the Heavy Artillery under his command and the Infantry.

   The B.G. Corps H.A. will ensure that the advantages of enfilade fire are fully made use of when possible—and he is responsible specially for complete liaison between the Artillery under his command and the Infantry.

7.   System of Counter Battery Work

   (a) The dividing line between the 1st and Canadian Corps for C.B. work will be the Southern edge of Square M : arrangements will be made direct between G.O.Cs.R.A. of Corps for overlap of fire into their respective areas.

        The dividing line between First and Third Armies will be an east and west line through the Southern edge of Square B.7.

(*b*) Each Counter Battery Group will contain one 4·5″ howitzer battery and one or more Heavy or Medium Howitzer batteries in addition to the 60-pdr. or 4·7″ batteries allotted to it.

So long as there is destructive work to be carried out on hostile batteries these Medium or Heavy Howitzer batteries will not be available for other work.

If the hostile batteries located in the theatre of operations become greatly increased in number it may be necessary to make use of some of the batteries allotted to Divisional fronts for trench destruction, to reinforce the C.B. Groups : where such necessity arises very early notice should be given to Commanders of Siege Artillery in the Sectors concerned in order not to interfere with the programme of trench destruction more than necessary.

(*c*) As there will be two flights allotted to each Corps for C.B. work, the Corps C.B. area should be divided into two, a C.B. Group being allotted to each area for normal work, the third C.B. Group will be available for reinforcement in either area. Special attention must be paid to taking full advantage of enfilade fire : it is the duty of the Lt.-Colonel for C.B. work to arrange this.

(*d*) Counter Battery work will be carried out continuously up to 10 days before the " zero " day, in accordance with the accepted principles, namely, that active hostile batteries accurately located will be destroyed as soon as possible, a sufficiency of ammunition being expended to carry out the work thoroughly.

(*e*) The policy during the 10 days previous to " zero " day will be as follows :

The work of destruction will be carried on with the greatest vigour, the ruling principle being that isolated active batteries will be dealt with first and those collected into groups or nests will be reserved for destruction to the last. It is easier to neutralize such groups, both with H.E. and Gas Shell, than isolated batteries. It must be clearly understood, however, that any particularly active and offensive hostile battery must be destroyed as soon as possible whether in a group or not, and also that the destruction of groups must not be postponed if no other work is waiting to be done.

A very effective method of neutralizing the hostile artillery is to destroy their telephone exchanges : these should be marked down and destroyed by very short concentrated bombardments at the latest possible moment before the attack is launched.

Similarly the destruction of O.Ps. should be reserved to the latest possible moment, arrangements being made for blinding those groups of O.Ps. with smoke clouds from 18-pr. and other shell which cannot be destroyed in a short bombardment.

(*f*) At the opening of the Infantry attack the policy of destruction must give way to one of neutralization. As every effort will be made to make the opening of the attack a surprise, the amount of neutralizing fire [which] will be opened will depend on the observations made as to time of opening

E

fire of hostile barrage batteries, during such feint attacks as are made during the preliminary bombardment, e.g. if it can be deduced from these observations that the enemy takes 6 minutes to open their barrage, neutralizing fire might be started at 0 + 5.

When once the neutralizing fire opens, however, every hostile position known to be occupied will be brought under the intense fire as far as this is possible with the means at our disposal.

It is better to bring a heavy fire from 2 guns or howitzers on one battery position than to attempt to neutralize two batteries with a single gun each.

As, however, at this stage many of the Siege batteries originally allotted for trench destruction will be set free and become available for C.B. work, it should be possible to bring heavy neutralizing fire on all known positions.   The intensity of this neutralizing fire will diminish after a quarter of an hour, and the work of destruction of batteries will again be taken up as opportunity offers.

As far as possible this neutralizing fire will be controlled by air and ground observers : the former must be fully conversant with the plan arranged for this work.

Special attention must be paid to the selection of batteries for neutralizing with gas shells : those nests of batteries not completely destroyed will be specially marked down for treatment in this way.

The efficacy of the gas shells will depend on a proper appreciation of the atmospheric conditions, especially of the wind ; at the opening of a bombardment with gas shells fire must be intense and concentrated : after a thick cloud of gas has been formed the rate of fire should be reduced and H.E. shell interspersed.   Occasional return to heavy concentrated bursts of gas shells will tend to keep low the efficiency of the hostile batteries concerned.

The effect of this method of neutralization must be closely watched, so that if it has met with marked success it may be applied to other nests of batteries, after one has been silenced.

After zero, the fullest possible use must be made by the I Corps of the Divisional Artillery covering the defensive front from the Double Crassier southwards for neutralizing the hostile artillery.

(g) The capture of the final objective which will afford us observation over the Douai plain, and the success of the two Southern Divisions will compel the hostile batteries over a large portion of the front concerned to fall back. In order that Counter Battery work may be effectively carried out after the capture of the final objective a large number of the batteries of the C.B. groups will have to move forward to a very appreciable extent.

The general scheme for this movement must be carefully thought out, the details being all arranged and issued to the units concerned in the form of a table showing the batteries that will have to move, their new positions, the order in which they will move, &c.

The new positions must where possible be stocked with ammunition beforehand.

8. The Preliminary Bombardment

(*a*) Although the main preliminary bombardment will only last 48 hours, 3 to 4 weeks previous to this the work of destruction will be commenced, care being taken to disguise as far as possible the fact that a large concentration of Artillery has taken place. The batteries that have been in position for some considerable time will be used for this.

(*b*) As ground observation is difficult in many parts of the theatre of operations the objectives to be destroyed prior to the opening of the main bombardment must be those which cannot be seen, or can only be seen with difficulty, from the ground, and require aerial observation. This will ease the programme of destructive work to be carried out with aerial observation during the main bombardment, and enable close examination of photographs showing the effect, to be made. Careful organization is required to ensure that any works destroyed both during this period and later are kept under the fire of Field guns so as to prevent any work of repair being carried out.

(*c*) During the period of preparation a table will have been made out, of all points which require destruction before the assault can take place : with this as a basis the programme of bombardment should be made out. Whole trench systems cannot be destroyed : fire must be concentrated on the important points such as trench junctions, m.g. emplacements, &c. Similarly neither woods nor villages should be bombarded as a whole : fire must be directed on to those portions which are to be attacked or which will afford observation, or threaten the flank of an attack.

Very careful organization will be required to ensure that there is no loss of time in such cases where aerial observation is required, and that the vicinity of the points that are being bombarded with such observation is kept as clean as possible of other shell fire to avoid confusing the observer.

(*d*) Commanders must, during the preparatory period, give constant attention to increasing the number of rounds of observed fire than can be fired during the flight of a single airman : the satisfactory completion of the programme of destruction depends very largely on the factor of time.

(*e*) Good and continuous observation is the key to successful destruction : after careful registration, fire for effect will take place at a steady rate of fire, controlled either by the observer who carried out the registration, or possibly by a second observer who has been following the registration : (possibly also from a balloon).

(*f*) Medium and Heavy Trench mortars must be used to their full extent to relieve the Siege Batteries from the work of destruction on the front system as far as possible.

(*g*) It must be fully appreciated that if the enemy concentrates such a force of Artillery in the theatre of operations as to require the fire of more batteries than are available in the C.B. groups, some of the Siege Batteries now allotted for trench destruction will be placed at the disposal of one or more of these C.B. Groups. Such a possibility must be foreseen in arranging the programme of destruction.

(*h*) Arrangements must be made to prepare the way for the Infantry to advance to the final objective on the day of assault, so that they may be able to reap the full benefit of a complete breakdown of the defence. It will not be possible to cut the wire along the whole front of the strong line running N. and S. through Thélus, but gaps must be cut by concentrations of fire from Field and Medium Howitzers using 106 fuzes : the site for these gaps must be carefully selected in consultation with the General Staff and maps prepared and distributed down to Company Commanders showing where the gaps will be.

The destruction of Thélus will be carried out by means of the heaviest possible concentration of fire and during the latter part of the preliminary bombardment, arrangements must also be made to bring this concentrated fire to bear immediately before the Infantry assault the place.

If it is not found possible to make gaps in the new wire entanglements between Thélus and the Farbus Wood during the preliminary bombardment, at zero the fire of several howitzer batteries must be concentrated with a view to making gaps at selected places.

(*i*) Throughout the hours of darkness during the main preliminary bombardment all the known lines of approach to the front system of trenches will be kept under constant harassing fire of considerable intensity ; no reliefs, or ration or ammunition parties should be able to reach the front line without suffering heavily : heavy guns should also search the rearward approaches, and refilling points, etc. with special attention to the approaches to all known hostile positions.

(*j*) As the majority of the batteries will be firing continuously night and day special arrangements must be made for the relief of the personnel : all ranks must be given a sufficiency of rest if they are to maintain their efficiency during a long period of operations.

The guns of all batteries must also be rested, and overhauled on a carefully thought-out plan : it should rarely be necessary for all guns of a battery to be firing at the same time.

(*k*) During the preliminary bombardment arrangements will be made for a rehearsal of the opening phase of the attack as far as the artillery is concerned : this will take place at a time, and under conditions, that will be laid down by A.H.Q. : during this rehearsal observation will be carried out by specially selected officers for the purpose of (1) Correcting any mistakes in the arrangements such as gaps in the barrage fire, (2) For locating the positions and density of the hostile barrage.

A similar rehearsal will take place of the barrages that will cover the attack on the I Corps front, at a time which will be determined by A.H.Q.

(*l*) Arrangements will be made for aeroplane photographs to be taken of the bombarded areas at times which will be ordered from A.H.Q. A study of these photographs will form a guide to the issue or orders for the following day.

(m) No increase in the rate of fire will be made as zero hour approaches, in order that the attack may come as a surprise.

(n) Shortly before, at, or shortly after zero a number of Medium and Heavy Howitzers will probably be placed at the disposal of the various Counter Battery Group Commanders. Decision on this question cannot be made until the Hostile Artillery situation at the time, and the habits of their barrage batteries, have been appreciated.

(o) The importance of correctly estimating the error of the day must be appreciated, and opportunity given to batteries to fire on their Datum points. This requires careful arrangements, and must be carried out on zero day if the plan admits of it.

9. Barrages

In arranging the programme of lifts and barrages during the attack, simplicity must be the key-word. As far as possible the area will be divided into channels down which the fire of Brigades of Artillery will creep.

Whether Time or Percussion Shrapnel is used for the creeping barrage must depend on the conditions under which the assault is to take place.

Again, the rate of advance of this barrage depends on the state of the ground, and the number of trenches to be crossed.

Both the rate of advance, and the halts for re-forming of the Infantry will be co-ordinated by A.H.Q. according to plans of the Third Army. Maps showing the rate of advance of the creeping barrages and the halts must be issued to the Infantry down as far as Company Commanders.

As a general principle there will be a standing barrage in advance of the creeping barrage which will be composed of 4·5″ howitzers and a proportion of 18-pdrs. : these latter will occasionally search and sweep within narrow limits to prevent the occupants of the trenches on which this barrage is established from occupying shell holes in advance or in rear of them.

10. Support of Infantry in later stages

The arrangements for the forward move of Field and Siege Artillery requires most careful organization. The new positions must be selected, and where possible, prepared, and ammunition placed ready in them. The same procedure as regards tables showing the plan must be drawn up, as is laid down in para. 7 (System of Counter Battery Work).

The necessity for bridging trenches where required must be foreseen : and the work completed before the preliminary bombardment, where possible.

11. 12″ and 15″ Howitzers

These are being retained under the Command of G.O.C. R.A. of the First Army. They will mainly be used for

C.B. work, and destructive bombardments. As regards the former, Corps will call directly on the O.C. 26th Heavy Artillery Group for fire ; the ammunition allotted for this work will be notified to Corps from time to time.

If Corps wish to use these heavy howitzers for any special tasks, application must be made to G.O.C. R.A. First Army.

12. R.F.C.

It is of very great importance that G.O.Cs. R.A. of Corps should communicate their plans as early as possible to O.C., 1st Wing R.F.C., to enable him to make his arrangements : constant touch between these two is essential.

FIFTH ARMY PLAN OF OPERATIONS, S.G. 672, 16TH FEBRUARY 1917

1.   In accordance with the instructions contained in your O.A.D. 300 of the 30th January 1917, a further plan of operations is forwarded herewith.

2.   Owing to the capture of Grandcourt, the situation has somewhat changed since my G.Z. 35 of the 30th January was submitted for the approval of the Commander-in-Chief, and there is difficulty in discovering where the enemy's real line of resistance now is.

There are certain indications that no very serious opposition will be encountered before reaching the Achiet-le-Petit—Loupart Wood line ; and it is quite possible that even that line will only be held as an advanced position to the Bihucourt line (see map 1 attached) upon which a great deal of labour has recently been expended.

3.   It is therefore proposed that the main operations of the Fifth Army should be directed towards breaking the Achiet-le-Petit—Loupart Wood line and gaining position for the attack upon the Bihucourt line.

It is suggested that this operation should take place upon Z – 3 day, and carried through in one day.

The Bihucourt line is heavily wired and my present information leads me to believe that I shall not be able to get observation on to it until I am in possession of Loupart Wood.   Ammunition supply for wire cutting is also likely to be difficult, so that it is possible that there will be some delay before I can renew the attack.

These attacks to be followed as quickly as possible by an advance in the direction of St. Leger in accordance with your instructions.

This is a considerably more ambitious scheme than that previously submitted, but it is considered that the changed situation justifies me in making the attempt.

4.   Before this main attack, i.e. against Achiet-le-Petit—Loupart Wood, can be delivered it will be necessary to carry out a series of minor operations, principally with a view to gaining the necessary gun positions.

The scope of these successive operations, and the dates upon which it is proposed to carry them out, are indicated on the attached map 2.

They are :—

(a)   Capture of Hill 130, South of Pys, by II Corps, 17th February.

(b)   Capture of Butte de Warlencourt and Gird Trench by Anzac Corps, 1st March.

(c)   Capture of Serre by V Corps, 7th March.

(d)   After capture of Serre, the V Corps will extend its right to the River Ancre, thereby enabling the II Corps to withdraw the 63rd Division for further training.

(e)   Capture of Miraumont by V Corps, 10th March.

(f)   Capture of Bois Loupart and the Achiet-le-Petit—Loupart Wood line on the front shown on the map, by II Corps and Anzac Corps, Z – 3.

One and a half to two Australian Divisions would take part in this operation.

5.   It is not considered desirable to attempt this last operation earlier than Z – 3, as weather or any other cause may possibly delay the operations of the Third Army.

Also, by leaving more than three days between operation (f) and Third Army operations, we might give the enemy time, not only to check us, but to realize that he had succeeded in doing so. He would then be free to meet the fresh danger from the North.

6.   It is not at present possible to foresee what troops will be able to push forward towards St. Leger, but the necessity for doing so will be borne in mind throughout the earlier operations.

H. P. Gough,
General,
Commanding Fifth Army.

TELEGRAPHIC ORDERS BY V CORPS

7th, 19th, 11th, 31st, 62nd Divns., G.O.C.R.A.,
Fifth Army, II Corps, XVIII Corps, Nos. 5 &
15 Sqdns. R.F.C., V Corps Mtd. Tps., Intelligence,
Q., C.E., D.D.M.S.   G. 301.   24th (February).
Indications point to the enemy having retired along the whole front
of the V Corps, and touch has been lost.   Touch with the enemy
will be obtained tonight.   All Divns. will at once push out patrols
to their front and arrange to bring up supporting troops.   In each
case the Brigade in immediate reserve will be ready to move at
short notice after 5 A.M. tomorrow.   At 5 A.M. tomorrow 62nd
Divn. will push strong advanced guards towards (a) Beauregard
Dovecote and (b) Puisieux.   7th Divn. will push strong advanced
guards towards (a) Pendant Alley and Wing Trench (b) Serre.   If
these places are found unoccupied advanced guards supported by
main body will push on to Puisieux.   19th Divn. will push out
strong patrols of at least a platoon each along the whole of their
front towards Serre and Star Wood.   31st Divn. will push out
strong patrols of at least a platoon each along their whole front
towards Rossignol Wood and Gommecourt.   All Divns. will occupy
all ground evacuated by the enemy and push strong supporting
bodies up behind their advanced guards and patrols.   Corps Mtd.
Tps. will move one troop to Mailly Maillet tonight.   Acknowledge.
Addsd. all concerned.
V Corps.

PROPOSED ORGANIZATION OF UNIFIED COMMAND ON THE WESTERN FRONT, 26TH FEBRUARY 1917

(TRANSLATION)

1.   By delegation of the British War Committee, with the assent of the French War Committee, and in order to ensure unity of command on the Western Front, the French General-in-Chief will, from the 1st March 1917, have authority over the British forces operating on this front, in all that concerns the conduct of operations, and especially :
— the planning and execution of offensive and defensive actions ;
— the dispositions of the forces by Armies and Groups of Armies ;
— the boundaries between these higher formations ;
— the allotment of material and resources of all natures to the Armies.

2.   The French Commander-in-Chief will have at his disposal a British Chief of the General Staff who will reside at the French G.Q.G.
This Chief of the General Staff will have under his orders :
(*a*) A General Staff entrusted with the study of questions concerning operations and the relations with the British War Committee ;
(*b*) The Quarter-Master General.
It will be his duty to keep the British War Committee in touch with the situation of the British Armies and to transmit to it the demands of the French Commander-in-Chief regarding the needs of these Armies.
He will transmit to the British Commander-in-Chief, to the Army commanders, or Army Group commanders operating independently, the directives and instructions of the French Commander-in-Chief.
Under the authority of the Chief of the General Staff, the Quarter-Master General will be entrusted with the distribution among the British Armies of resources of all natures, and with transmitting to the Director-General of Transport the instructions necessary to his services.

3.   Questions of personnel and general discipline in the British Armies will be dealt with by the British Commander-in-Chief, Army

commanders or Army Group commanders operating independently, and the British Chief of the General Staff, in accordance with powers which are allotted to him by the War Office.

4. The composition and functions of the British General Staff attached to the French Commander-in-Chief will be laid down by agreement between Field-Marshal Sir Douglas Haig and General Nivelle.

5. In case of the supersession of the French Commander-in-Chief his powers would pass to the new French Commander-in-Chief in default of a fresh decision of the two War Committees.

NOTE.—Among other comments in the hand-writing of Sir Douglas Haig on copies of this document is the following :—" (Proposal put " forward by M. Briand but withdrawn after discussion at Calais " 27 Feb. 1917)."

AGREEMENT SIGNED AT ANGLO - FRENCH CONFERENCE HELD AT CALAIS, 26TH/27TH FEBRUARY 1917

1. The French War Committee and the British War Cabinet approve of the plan of operations on the Western Front as explained to them by General Nivelle and Field-Marshal Sir Douglas Haig on February 26, 1917.

2. With the object of ensuring complete unity of command, during the forthcoming military operations referred to above, the French War Committee and the British War Cabinet have agreed to the following arrangements :—

(i) Whereas the primary object of the forthcoming military operations referred to in para. 1 is to drive the enemy from French soil, and whereas the French Army disposes of larger effectives than the British, the British War Cabinet recognizes that the general direction of the campaign should be in the hands of the French Commander-in-Chief :

(ii) With this object in view the British War Cabinet engages itself to direct the Field Marshal Commanding the British Expeditionary Force to conform his plans of operation to the general strategical plans of the Commander-in-Chief of the French Army :

(iii) The British War Cabinet further engages itself to direct that during the period intervening between the date of the signature of this agreement and the date of the commencement of the operation referred to in para. 1, the Field Marshal Commanding the British Expeditionary Force shall conform his preparations to the views of the Commander-in-Chief of the French Army, except in so far as he considers that this would endanger the safety of his army or prejudice its success ; and, in any case where Field Marshal Sir Douglas Haig may feel bound on these grounds to depart from General Nivelle's instructions, he shall report the action taken, together with the reasons for such action, to the Chief of the Imperial General Staff, for the information of the British War Cabinet :

(iv) The British War Cabinet further engages itself to instruct the Field Marshal Commanding the British Expeditionary Force that, after the date of the commencement of the forthcoming operations referred to in para. 1, and up to the termination of these operations, he shall conform to the orders of the Commander-in-Chief of the French Army in all matters relating to the conduct of the operations, it being understood that the British Commander will be left free to choose the means he will employ and the methods

of utilizing his troops in that sector of operations allotted to him
by the French Commander-in-Chief in the original plan.

(v) The British War Cabinet and Government and the French
Government, each so far as concerns its own Army, will be the judge
of the date at which the operations referred to in para. 1, are to be
considered as at an end.   When so ended the arrangement in force
before the commencement of the operations will be re-established.

BRIAND	D. LLOYD GEORGE
LYAUTEY	W. R. ROBERTSON, C.I.G.S.
R. NIVELLE	D. HAIG, F.M.

Calais,
    February 27, 1917.

NOTE.—On Sir Douglas Haig's copy there is a marginal note in
his handwriting :—" Signed by me as a correct statement, but not as
" approving the arrangement.   D. HAIG."

AGREEMENT BETWEEN FIELD - MARSHAL
SIR DOUGLAS HAIG AND GENERAL
NIVELLE ON THE APPLICATION OF
THE CALAIS CONVENTION OF THE
27TH FEBRUARY 1917, SIGNED 13TH
MARCH 1917

(TRANSLATION) [1]

I.

Relations between the French and British Commanders-in-Chief.

1.   The French Commander-in-Chief will only communicate with
the Authorities of the British Army through the British Commander-
in-Chief.   This arrangement does not apply to the relations between
neighbouring Groups of Armies or Armies, nor to the carrying out
of the duties of the French Mission such as they are at the present
time.

2.   The French Commander-in-Chief receives from the British Commander-in-Chief information as to his operation orders as well as all
information respecting their execution.

The operation orders of subordinate units are communicated to
one another by neighbouring units in conformity with the usual
custom, as required by the necessities of war.

3.   All the British troops stationed in France remain in all circumstances under the orders of their own chiefs and of the British
Commander-in-Chief.   If the development of the operations should
cause the French Commander-in-Chief to ask the British Commander-in-Chief to use a part of his forces for an action independent
of the rest of the British Army, the British Commander-in-Chief
will do his utmost to satisfy this demand.   The Commander of the
Forces thus detached may receive, as long as his independent position
lasts direct orders respecting operations from the French Higher
Command.

[1] In this case it has seemed right to give the translation made at the
time, though it is not particularly good, and had to be altered in respect
of one obscurity at the request of Sir Douglas Haig.   The note at the
foot by Sir Douglas Haig was written in English and is an integral part
of the document, being given (in English) in the copy published in the
French Official History.

II.

Duties of the British Mission attached to the French Headquarters.

1. As before, the object of the British Mission attached to the French Headquarters is to maintain touch between the French and British Commanders-in-Chief.

The French Commander-in-Chief can employ the members of the Mission in studying and in drawing up the instructions which are afterwards sent under his signature.

In principle, all instructions and communications sent to Sir Douglas Haig will be signed by General Nivelle. In case of absence or in an emergency, they may be signed by the Chief of the Staff or by the Chief of the British Mission acting by delegation of the French Commander-in-Chief.

2. The duties of the Chief of the British Mission at the French Headquarters are as follows :
(a) In respect of the British Commander-in-Chief.

To keep him informed of the intentions of the French Commander-in-Chief and to transmit to him his directions ; to keep him informed of the situation of the French Armies and the development of their operations ;

To keep him informed of the resources of every kind which the French Higher Command can place at the disposal of the British Armies, as well as of the period in which the demands of the British Higher Command can receive satisfaction ;
(b) In respect to the French Commander-in-Chief.

To keep him informed as to the general situation of the British Armies in France and as to the intentions of the Commander-in-Chief of these Armies ;

To keep him informed of the orders given to the British Armies in France for the preparation and execution of the plans of operations, as well as the way in which the operations are developing ;

To keep him informed in good time as to the material situation in every respect of the British Armies in France and as to their needs, in order that he may be able to satisfy the latter in so far as he is concerned.

The Chief of the Mission has under his orders two general officers charged, one with the study of questions of operations, the other with the study of questions respecting the administrative services, and a certain number of staff officers.

3. The General Officer, charged under the direction of the Chief of the Mission, with questions of operations, will have as his particular duty, to study in detail the plans and orders of operations and to follow their execution, so as to be able to supply his chief with the necessary information for the accomplishment of his task, both with respect to the French Higher Command and with respect to the British Higher Command.

He will keep in constant touch with the Third Bureau of the French General Staff and with the Operations Section of the British General Staff.

4. The General Officer charged, under the direction of the Chief

of the Mission, with questions concerning administrative services, has the duty :

of knowing the resources and the needs of the British Armies as well as the means placed at their disposal by the French Higher Command, and in particular, transport and labour ;

Of foreseeing in good time the problem relating to those questions which may arise from the development of operations, and of studying their solution.

He will keep in constant touch on the one hand with the French D.A. and on the other hand with the British Quarter-Master General and Director of Transport.

5. The Staff Officers attached to the aforesaid General Officers will be charged with the work of the Staff and with the " liaison " which their respective Missions entail.

London, 13th March 1917.   R. NIVELLE.

I agree with the above on the understanding that, while I am fully determined to carry out the Calais Agreement in spirit and letter, the British Army and its Commander-in-Chief will be regarded by General Nivelle as Allies and not as subordinates, except during the particular operations which he explained at the Calais Conference.

Further, while I also accept the Agreement respecting the functions of the British Mission at French Headquarters, it should be understood that these functions may be subject to modifications as experience shows to be necessary.

D. HAIG,
F.M.

BATTLES OF ARRAS

THIRD ARMY APPRECIATION AND INSTRUCTIONS, No. G.S. 1/37, 14TH MARCH 1917

The following changes have taken place during the last month :—

1.   The German divisions facing the Fifth Army have withdrawn their front to Bapaume, Bucquoy, Monchy.

Prisoners' statements, the destruction of villages, the removal of huts and the movement of guns, indicate that the above front is only lightly held, and that the bulk of the German forces have already withdrawn to about the Hindenburg Line between Hermies and St. Leger.

2.   The effect of these changes on the situation immediately in front of the proposed attack of the Third Army is that the reserves of the German forces, facing our Fifth Army, are probably now situated, or will be, in positions some 5 or 10 miles behind the Hindenburg Line ; that is to say, in the area between that line and the Scarpe.

3.   The German artillery is now also probably behind that line, and the guns which can bear on our attack are probably already considerably more numerous than was the case a month ago.

4.   The operations of the Third Army will now be an advance directed on Cambrai, with the object of turning the German defensive line which runs from Arras to St. Quentin.

5. (a) The general situation and the scope of operations already arranged for the VI. Corps will remain unaltered.

(b) The operations of the VII. Corps are dependent on the situation of the Germans at the time that operations begin :—

The following situation must be considered :

i.   The situation as it presents itself now, in which case the plans already prepared will hold good.

ii.   The situation that would arise, should the Germans be occupying with delaying detachments only the area Beaurains, Croisilles, Ransart, while their main defensive front runs along the line Tilloy-lez-Mofflaines, western and southern borders of The Harp, Neuville-Vitasse, the high ground south of Héninel.

F

In this eventuality, the first operation of the VII. Corps will be to press back the enemy's delaying detachments to their main line of defence. This operation will probably be assisted by the Fifth Army.

Artillery positions and observation will be secured in the area about Mercatel, in order to assist the assault on the German main line by the VII. Corps, and to enfilade the German third line between Feuchy Chapel and Feuchy, and bring a concentrated fire on Monchy-le-Preux.

The second operation of the VII. Corps will consist of the capture of the German main line from the high ground south of Héninel, to the centre of The Harp.

iii.   The situation which would be presented should the Germans have fallen back entirely to their main line of defence prior to the date of the main operations.

Under this condition, the action of the VII. Corps would be as described in para. 5(*b*) ii, except that the first operation would consist merely in the occupation of the ground evacuated by the enemy.

iv.   The situation which would result if, on the day of the main operation, the Germans should, although presenting a strong front to the last, fall back rapidly on being attacked to their main line.

In this case, the VII. Corps must be prepared to pivot rapidly on its left, bring all its artillery to new positions about Mercatel, and commence the assault of the main German line as rapidly as possible. At the same time, it will probably be necessary for the VII. Corps to cover its right flank.

v.   In the situations described under sub-paras. 5(*b*) iii and iv, and possibly under that described in sub-para. 5(*b*) ii, the VII. Corps may be able to carry out the operations described without engaging its reserve division. This division will, under these circumstances, be held in Army reserve.

(c) The operations of the XVII. Corps will remain as already arranged up to the capture of the Brown Line. Except that, should the operations of the VII. Corps diminish in scope as described in sub-paras. 5(*b*) ii, iii, and iv, a proportion [1] of guns of all natures will be transferred from the VII. Corps to the XVII. Corps. The XVII. Corps must, therefore, now make preparations to receive and use a number of guns approximately greater by one third than the numbers already allotted.

In this case, after the capture of the Brown Line, the XVII. Corps will be prepared to push through two divisions instead of one division, with the object of gaining rapidly the line Estrées, Vitry-en-Artois, Oppy.

The additional division allotted for this purpose to the XVII. Corps will be drawn from the Army reserve (XVIII. Corps), and may be replaced in the XVIII. Corps by the reserve division of the VII. Corps.

6.   The preparation for the employment of the Cavalry Corps will remain unaltered.

---

[1] If, however, additional guns become available from elsewhere, this transfer will not be necessary.

The Cavalry Corps and attached infantry division will be prepared to act north and south of the Scarpe as in the plan already issued.

It must, however, be recognized that owing to the greater concentration of German reserves in the area north of the Cojeul Switch or Hindenburg Line, it may not be possible to employ the Cavalry Corps usefully so early in the operations, and that it may therefore be necessary to employ the XVIII. Corps in breaking the German formations east of Monchy-le-Preux before employing the Cavalry Corps.

7.   Dependent on the above, the XVIII. Corps will be prepared either to follow closely on the VI. Corps with the object of securing the line Quéant, Vitry-en-Artois, or to follow the Cavalry Corps and to force its way to Cambrai.

Owing to the intention of securing more ground north of the Scarpe than was previously intended, it is possible that lines of advance for the XVIII. Corps, other than those south of the Scarpe, will become available.

The XVIII. Corps will, therefore, be prepared to make use of the following roads in addition to those already reconnoitred south of the Scarpe :—

    i. The Blangy—Feuchy—Pelves road.
    ii. The Scarpe canal towpath.
    iii. The Laurent-Blangy, Fampoux, Plouvain road.
    iv. The Laurent-Blangy, Gavrelle, Plouvain road.
    v. The Laurent-Blangy, Gavrelle, St. Vaast road.

L. J. Bols.
Major-General,
General Staff, Third Army.

G.H.Q. LETTER O.A.D. 337,
16TH MARCH 1917

To

General Sir H. S. Horne, K.C.B.,
  Commanding First Army.
General Sir H. C. O. Plumer, G.C.M.G., K.C.B.,
  Commanding Second Army.
General Sir E. H. H. Allenby, K.C.B.,
  Commanding Third Army.
General Sir H. S. Rawlinson, Bt., K.C.B., K.C.V.O.,
  Commanding Fourth Army.
General Sir H. de la P. Gough, K.C.B.,
  Commanding Fifth Army.
Lt.-General Sir C. T. McM. Kavanagh, K.C.B., C.V.O., D.S.O.,
  Commanding Cavalry Corps.

1.   Available evidence points to the probability of the enemy's withdrawal being continued, whether under pressure of the allied troops or otherwise, as far as the Hindenburg Line (Arras—St. Quentin—Laon).

It is not yet clear whether the objects the enemy has in view are or are not as suggested in O.A.D. 329, dated the 9th March.[1]

2.   The general intention of the Field-Marshal Commanding-in-Chief is :—

(a)   To maintain pressure on the enemy and harass his rear guards with the minimum number of troops required for that purpose.

(b)   To strike the enemy on the Arras—Vimy front in the greatest possible strength with a view to penetrating his defences, outflanking the Hindenburg line from the north, and operating in the direction of Cambrai.

Advantage should be taken of local opportunities to cause the enemy loss in his retirement, especially by means of artillery fire ; but attacks in force, which will be met by rear guards fully prepared,

---

[1] It was there stated that the enemy presumably hoped by his retreat—
    (a) to render useless preparations already made for an allied offensive on that front, compelling the Allies to recommence them, and thus gaining time to develop his own plans ;
    (b) to utilize the time so gained and the troops thereby made available for an offensive on a great scale.   (Compiler's note.)

are unlikely under the conditions to give an adequate return for the losses likely to be incurred. They should only be resorted to for some special and adequate object and should be well prepared and supported by artillery.

3. The Fourth Army will cooperate with the Fifth Army on its left and with the French on its right, covering the flank of each in any advance they make. It will follow up (on the lines laid down in para. 2 above) any retirement along its front, and will bear especially in mind the advantages of gaining possession of Mont St. Quentin.

The dividing lines will be as follows :—

Between the French and Fourth Army : Roye—Nesle— Ham, all inclusive to the French.

Between the Fourth and Fifth Armies : Le Transloy— Barastre—Bertincourt—Havrincourt Wood, all inclusive to the Fourth Army.

4. The Fifth Army, while combining its action with the Fourth Army, will pay special attention to the necessity for close co-operation between its left and the right of the Third Army. In order to facilitate the operations of the Third Army, the Fifth Army will aim at establishing Artillery on the general line Beugny— Mory— Hamelincourt as early as possible so as to bring the German defences of the Hindenburg Line under fire from the south.

The dividing line between the Third and Fifth Armies will remain as at present.

5. The operations of the Third Army after breaking through the enemy's defences on the front of attack will be directed with a view to capturing the German defensive line which runs from Arras towards St. Quentin by turning it and attacking it in flank and rear, continuing to operate in the direction of Cambrai.

Since it is improbable that there will be any considerable hostile forces in the salient south of Arras, the instructions contained in O.A.D. 260, dated the 2nd January, are modified accordingly.

6. The First Army will carry out the orders already issued, with the following modification. The XIII Corps, consisting of 3 divisions, will be transferred from the Fifth Army to the First Army in augmentation of the forces already allotted to the latter. This Corps will be regarded as a reserve available primarily to enable the First Army to exploit any success and operate in the direction of Douai and thus to cover the left of the Third Army advancing on Cambrai : but also available, in whole or part, according to developments, either to reinforce the Third Army in the exploitation of successes gained or to reinforce the Second Army.

7. After the arrival of the 19th Division the Second Army will maintain 3 divisions in reserve.

Second Army will study and report what action is possible in the direction of Langemarck with the troops available and in co-operation with the Belgian Army in the event of the enemy being defeated elsewhere and thus being compelled to weaken himself on the Belgian and Second Army fronts.

The preparations for the Messines—Wytschaete attack will be continued.

8. Zero day for the Arras—Vimy attacks has already been communicated verbally to the First and Third Armies. Every effort will be made to complete the preparations so that the full programme can be carried out.

9. As the situation develops it is intended gradually to withdraw divisions from the Fourth and Fifth Armies as shown on Diagram A attached.

G.H.Q. reserves will then be formed on or about Z day (under orders to be issued later by the Commander-in-Chief) as follows :—

> In First Army area :   1 Corps—2 Divisions.
> In Fourth Army area : 1 Corps—2 Divisions.

10. The movement of troops required to complete the concentration is shewn on the attached papers summarised below. (The Table issued under O.A.D. 309, dated the 8th February, is cancelled.) Separate orders have been or will be issued for each set of moves shewn on the Tables.

> (i) Diagram shewing the grouping of reserves and their probable movements, marked A.
> (ii) Table shewing the Artillery units (other than Divisional Artilleries) to be transferred, marked B.[1]
> (iii) Table shewing the general movement of concentration for the Arras—Vimy operations, marked C.[1]

L. E. KIGGELL,
Lieut.-General,
Chief of the General Staff.

[1] Not printed.

Diagram of concentration of Reserves A.

SECRET.

	SECOND (13)

23
25
19

G.H.Q. RESERVE
→ Steenbecque
↗ St. Hilaire
II

XIII
A or 31
B or 63
(D)

First
(13) + (2)
(in G.H.Q. Reserve)

Commence 31 March (by Rail)
Commence 31 March (by Rail)

20-27 March

Complete movement by 31 March

XVIII
C or 11
29
30
33

17
1 Cav.
2 Cav.
3 Cav.

THIRD
(18)

(A) (B) (D)

23 March or as soon as can be received

26-29 March

29 March - 4 April

FIFTH
(6)

(E) (F)

(C)

ARTY.
INF.

G.H.Q. RESERVE
(I)
(G) XIV

FOURTH
(9) + (2)
(in G.H.Q. Reserve)

TOTAL   63 divisions
includes PORTUGUESE
and 42nd.

BATTLES OF ARRAS

WARNING IN CASE OF ENEMY'S RETREAT, 19TH MARCH 1917

XVII Corps.[1]
  You are to be prepared to attack on the original plan at any time from now onwards at twenty-four hours' notice.

L. J. BOLS, Major-General,
8 P.M.   General Staff, Third Army.

  [1] A similar order was addressed to the other corps, in each case in the hand-writing of Major-General Bols.

BATTLES OF ARRAS

THIRD ARMY PLAN FOR ATTACK AT SHORT NOTICE, No. G.S. 1/42, 21ST MARCH 1917

With reference to instructions to be prepared to attack at short notice :—

1.   Preparations for " Z " day will continue as arranged.

2.   If attack is ordered at short notice, arrangements are now to be made to ensure that wire is cut to enable the Black Line to be occupied at 24 hours' notice.

3.   If the attack is ordered at short notice, the VII Corps will not be required to attack frontally in a north-easterly direction, but the VII Corps will be ready to co-operate on the right of the VI Corps.

C. J. C. GRANT, Lt.-Colonel,
General Staff, Third Army.

BATTLES OF ARRAS

2ND CANADIAN DIVISION INSTRUCTIONS FOR THE OFFENSIVE, No. 3, 24TH MARCH 1917

Less Appendix C

NOTE : Owing to change of plan, Instructions Nos. 1 and 2 are cancelled : those portions of the previous instructions, which are still relevant, are repeated in No. 3.

REFERENCE : Maps A 1/10,000 and B 1/20,000 and Tracing C already issued, and Map D 1/10,000 attached.[1]

1.   The Canadian Corps has been ordered to take the Vimy Ridge in conjunction with a larger operation by the Third Army. The 1st Canadian Division is attacking on the right, and the 3rd Canadian Division on the left of the 2nd Canadian Division, to whom the 13th (British) Brigade is attached.

2.   The boundaries of the 2nd Canadian Division are (vide Map D) :—

Southern Boundary :

From A.10.a.6½.0 along Mercier (inclusive) to the junction with Territorial Avenue, thence along Vistula (inclusive) to Claudot (exclusive), thence West along Claudot (exclusive) and Deep Valley Ditch to Bethune Road in A.14.a.   Thence as in Map B.

Northern Boundary :

Junction De la Fourche Trench with Front Line (A.4.a.4.5½) Westerly along De la Fourche (inclusive) to Parallel VIII.   Thence to road junction at A.3.Central, thence Southwesterly along the road and tramline to road junction at A.3.c.5.1 to road junction at A.3.c.4.2. Thence Southwesterly along road to road junction A.9.a.1.9½, along tramline to A.8.b.1.6½ to junction of Roy and Bethune Roads.   Road boundary West of A.3.Central (exclusive).   Thence as in Map B.   Dugouts in Chepstow at A.3.c.4½.1½ inclusive to 2nd Canadian Division.

[1] Not reproduced.

In addition a portion of the 3rd Canadian Division area (as shown in Green on Map D) has been placed at the disposal of this Division for the purpose of assembling the 13th Brigade.

3. The operation will be carried out in four phases : the first two phases, which are completed in the capture of the Red Line, being carried out by Brigades in front line : the second two phases, which are completed by the capture of the Brown Line, being carried out by Brigades in second line. (Vide Map D.)

The advance will be timed as follows :—

Line	Infantry reach at (i.e. barrage lifts off)	Infantry advance from at	Remarks
Black	Zero plus 32′	Zero plus 75′	(a) On Right of 4th Bde. at Zero plus 95′.
Red	Zero plus 103′ (a)	Zero plus 245′	
Blue	Zero plus 320′	Zero plus 424′ (b)	(b) On Southern Div. boundary only : Northern
Brown	Zero plus 468′	—	flank is stationary

4. (a) (Vide Map D.) The 1st Canadian Division is employing two Brigades for the first two phases (the 3rd Canadian Infantry Brigade being on our immediate right) and one Brigade (1st Canadian Infantry Brigade) for the second phase. The 3rd Brigade attacks with three Battalions in front line and one in reserve : the Battalions in front line going through to the Red Line. The 1st Brigade passes through the other two Brigades on the Red Line and advances to the Brown Line with three Battalions in front line.

1st Division Advanced Signal Centre will be at Maison Blanche.
3rd Bde. Report Centre at A.9.d.8.1 ⎫ at the com-
3rd Bde. Left Assaulting Bn. H.Q. at A.10.c.2½.3½ ⎪ mencement
1st Bde. Report Centre at A.15.b.9½.1 ⎬ of the
1st Bde. Left Assaulting Bn. H.Q. at A.15.b.2.1 ⎭ operations.

(b) (Vide Map D.) The 3rd Canadian Division is employing two Brigades for the first two phases (the 8th Canadian Infantry Brigade being on our immediate left) and one Brigade in Divisional Reserve. The 8th Brigade attacks with three Battalions in front line and one in Reserve : the Battalions in front line going through to the Red Line.

3rd Division Advanced Report Centre will be at F.6.c.5.5.
8th Bde. Report Centre at S.27.d.6.4.
1st C.M.R. (Right Assaulting Bn.) H.Q. at . . .

The Red Line of the 3rd Canadian Division includes the group of dugouts along the road from S.29.d.8.5 to S.30.a.6.2.

The Bois de Bonval is inclusive to the 3rd Canadian Division, who are responsible for keeping touch with this Division by establishing posts in the wood as we advance from the Red to the Blue Line : the 3rd Canadian Division will have a post about S.30.Central as soon as we have reached the Blue Line,

5. (*a*)   The 2nd Canadian Division will attack with the 4th and
5th Canadian Infantry Brigades in first line, and the 6th Canadian
and 13th (British) Brigades in second line.   (Vide Map D.)
(*b*)   The 4th Canadian Infantry Brigade on the right and the
5th Canadian Infantry Brigade on the left will have the Red
Line as their final objective.   Each Brigade is attacking with
two Battalions in front line, one Battalion in reserve and one
Battalion broken up for Moppers Up and carrying parties.
          The leading waves of the Battalions in front line will
go straight through to their objective, the Black Line, leaving
Mopping Up parties to deal with intervening trenches.
          The Reserve Battalions of each Brigade will follow its
leading Battalions and will pass through them on the Black Line,
where it will re-form and then recommence its advance ;   the
leading waves of these Reserve Battalions will go straight through
to their objective, the Red Line, leaving Mopping Up parties as
required.
(*c*) (i)   The 6th Canadian Infantry Brigade on the right and the
13th British Brigade on the left will have the Blue and Brown
Lines including the enemy's guns in the Bois de la Ville, Goulot
Wood and Bois du Goulot, as their objectives.   They will time
their advance from their positions of assembly (Zero plus two
hours is suggested) so as to reach the Red Line in sufficient time
to recommence their advance from that line at Zero plus two
hundred and forty five minutes.
(ii)   The 6th Canadian Infantry Brigade is attacking with
three Battalions in front line and one Battalion in Reserve ;
the three leading Battalions in front line going straight through
to the Blue Line, leaving Mopping Up parties as required.
          The advance from the Blue to the Brown Line is being
carried out by the Reserve Battalion which passes through the
leading Battalions on the Blue Line.
(iii)   The 13th (British) Brigade is attacking with two
Battalions in front line, one Battalion in support and one
Battalion in reserve.   The leading Battalions will push straight
through to the Blue Line which is the final objective of this
Brigade except for a small portion of Goulot Wood.   This
portion will be occupied by the 13th (British) Brigade when
the 6th Canadian Infantry Brigade resumes its advance from
the Blue to the Brown Line.
(iv)   In the event of either of the leading Brigades failing to
capture the Red Line, the 6th and 13th Brigades will be called
upon to undertake this before commencing their advance to the
Blue Line.
          In order not to break up the organization of the leading
Battalions, it is suggested that the Reserve Battalion of the 6th
Brigade and the Support Battalion of the 13th Brigade should
be employed for the capture of the Red Line, the original leading
Battalions being held back for their allotted task, the Blue
Line.
          Should the eventuality arise, the barrage will be brought
back after it has reached the Red Line and the new assault will
be launched under cover of a fresh creeping barrage.
          G.O.'sC. 6th and 13th Brigades will have plans prepared
to meet this situation and will practise this attack.

(*d*)   As the Divisional Commander will have no Reserves in hand, it is most important that the leading Battalions and the Mopping Up Battalions of the 4th and 5th Canadian Infantry Brigades should be collected and reorganized at the earliest possible moment in order to provide a reserve for eventualities.

(*e*)   At Zero the shrapnel barrage will begin and all assaulting troops of the 4th and 5th Canadian Infantry Brigades will leave their trenches and advance over the top of the ground to their objectives (a note as to the best method of overcoming the obstacles formed by the craters is attached as Appendix " A ") ; only Battalion H.Q., Signallers, Runners and wounded being allowed to use the trenches.

The advance of the 6th Canadian and 13th British Brigades from their assembly positions will be made similarly over the top of the ground.

Bridges over our trenches and guide posts will be fixed to enable troops in rear to move over the top.

4th and 5th Brigades will be responsible for the removal of wire in front of our front and support trenches, where necessary, due regard being paid to the concealment of this from the enemy until the last moment.

5th Brigade will also be responsible for cutting gaps in the wire in front of Parallel VIII ; details being arranged direct with G.O.'sC. 6th and 13th Brigades.

(*f*)   It must be thoroughly impressed on all ranks of the assaulting infantry that their success and safety lie in the leading wave following the barrage as closely as possible until their objective is gained.

The pace of the barrage up to the Red Line will be 100 yards in 3 minutes plus certain pauses for crossing trenches. From the Red Line to the Blue Line the pace will be 100 yards in 5 minutes without any pauses. From the Blue Line to the Brown Line the pace will be 100 yards in 4 minutes without any stops. A final barrage map will be issued shortly.

(*g*)   In the event of any Brigade, Battalion, Company or Platoon being held up, the units on the flanks will on no account check their advance, but will form defensive flanks towards the unit held up and press forward themselves so as to envelop the strong point or centre of resistance which is preventing the advance. With this object in view reserves will be pushed in behind those portions which are successful rather than those which are held up.

6. Brigade Boundaries (vide Map D).

(*a*)   The boundary between the 4th and 5th Brigades for all purposes will be :—
   Point A.5.d.4.6 on Red Line.
   Point A.5.c.5.6 on Black Line.
   Junction of Stafford Street and Front Line at A.4.d.1.4½.
   Stafford Street and Rietz Avenue as far West as A.10.a.1½.8½ (both common to both Brigades).
   Rietz Avenue to Bethune Road (inclusive to 5th Brigade).
   Lundy Island Redoubt except Rietz Avenue (inclusive to 4th Brigade).

(b)   The boundary between the 6th Canadian and 13th British Brigades for all purposes will be :—

Denis la Rocque (inclusive to 13th Brigade) from Bethune Road to Parallel VIII. Thence a straight line to junction of Balloon Avenue and Lille Road A.5.d.2½.9. Thence a straight line to junction of Telegrapher Weg and front line trench on Hill 140 (Farbus Line) A.6.d.5.6. Thence along Telegrapher Weg and track on North side of it (both inclusive to 6th Brigade) to Brown Line at B.1.d.½.9.

NOTE : The 13th Brigade will be permitted to use Rietz Avenue as their IN Trench.

7. Consolidation.

(a)   Every objective is to be consolidated immediately by the troops who have captured it, irrespective of whether other troops are passing through them or not.

The Black and Red Lines will continue to be held by 4th and 5th Brigades until orders are issued from Divisional Headquarters.   (See Para. 5 (d) above.)

(b)   Special Defence of Bois de Bonval Ravine.

Although the 3rd Canadian Division will ultimately have a post on the East side of the Ravine, the 5th Canadian Infantry Brigade must make special arrangements to protect its own left flank after the capture of the Red Line.   For this purpose one section machine guns, drawn from those machine guns originally employed as mobile guns (vide Appendix B Machine Gun Scheme, Para 3 (b) (ii) and (c) (iii)), and any Stokes Mortars which can be brought forward, should be posted in the vicinity of the junction of Dump Avenue and Lille Road.

(c)   The final scheme of consolidation (see Map D) will be as follows :—

(i)   An outpost line of detached posts running from the Southern Divisional Boundary just inside the Eastern edge of Bois de la Ville, thence through B.1.Central, including the group of dugouts in the road just South of this point, to road junction at T.25.c.4.2, thence along road to road junction at S.30.b.6½.0, and thence to S.30.Central where touch will be maintained with 3rd Division Post.   (See Para. 4 (b) above.)

On the 6th Brigade front those posts will be Lewis Gun posts only but on the 13th Brigade front, owing to the distance from (ii) below, those posts should consist of detached platoon posts, self-supporting and dug in in the best tactical position obtainable.   This line will eventually become the front line.

(ii)   An observation line running from Tax Trench (exclusive) along the line of German gun positions on the Western edges of the Bois de la Ville, Goulot Wood and Bois du Goulot to the Divisional boundary in the Bois de Bonval about S.30.c.8.8.

This line which is intended to cover all the O.P.s on the forward slopes of Hill 140 will ultimately become the support line.

All possible use will be made of the dugouts in the German gun positions, traverses being built as early as possible to protect the entrances of these dugouts from the East.

(iii)   A main line of resistance running just in rear of the crest of Hill 140.

Commencing on the Southern Divisional Boundary just North of Tax Trench, the line will run just West of the first line of wire as far as Tango Trench : from this point it will run South of Thélus Mill to the junction of Grenadier Graben and the Lille Road. Thence along Grenadier Graben for about 150 yards and thence across to Dump Avenue and the Northern Divisional Boundary about S.29.c.6.3, where it will connect up with 3rd Division Main Line, which will be Fickle Trench extended South from Prince Arnulf Graben to the Divisional Boundary. This line will be the reserve line : it must be sited with the greatest care, the essential point being that the trench is as near the crest of the ridge as possible without being exposed to view by the enemy to the North-east. A long field of fire is not essential. The line must be wired as soon as possible, the utmost use being made of existing German wire. Dugouts must also be provided as early as possible : it is hoped to obtain some assistance from a Tunnelling Company for this work. These dugouts will be used to accommodate the reserves on whose offensive action the defence of the ridge will mainly depend.

(iv)   A line of six strong points lettered U to Z about 400 yards apart and about 250 yards in rear of the Main Line. This line of strong points is intended to support the Main Line and to hold up any counter attack which might succeed in penetrating any part of the Main Line.

The strong points must be sited so as to cover the crest of the hill as far as possible, and also to provide mutual support to adjoining strong points. When completed each strong point will be manned by two machine guns and a platoon of not less than 20 rifles.

(v)   The 6th Canadian Infantry Brigade will be responsible for the consolidation of (i) (ii) and (iii) in their own area.

The 13th Brigade will be responsible for the consolidation of (i) and (ii) in their area and for (iii) from Telegrapher Weg to the Red Line.

The 5th Canadian Infantry Brigade will be responsible for (iii) from the Red Line to junction with 3rd Canadian Division.

Brigades concerned will be responsible for linking up with each other and also with Brigades on their outer flanks.

No Sapper or Pioneer assistance will be available for this consolidation.

Work will be commenced on the final consolidation scheme as quickly as possible after the various lines have been captured.

(vi)   The six strong points will be sited, constructed and wired by the Field Companies under the orders of the C.R.E. : work being commenced as soon as the situation permits. On completion they will be garrisoned as follows :—

U and V each { 1 Platoon 6th Brigade, 2 M.G.s 4th Brigade.

W and X each { 1 Platoon 13th Brigade, 2 M.G.s 4th Brigade.

Y and Z each { 1 Platoon 5th Brigade, 2 M.G.s 5th Brigade.

The platoons detailed as garrisons should be despatched

as early as possible to get in touch with the Engineer Officer detailed to construct the Strong Point and to assist the Engineer Party in the work of construction.

The Machine Guns will be found from the local defence guns of the 4th and 5th Brigades (vide Appendix " B " Machine Gun Scheme, Para. 3 (*c*) (iii) and (*d*) (iii)) : these guns will be got into position as soon as the Strong Point has been sited.

(vii)   As soon as 6th and 13th Brigades have gained their objectives, the mobile machine guns with these Brigades will be disposed so as to cover all the ground between the crest of the ridge and the observation line.

(*d*)   Communication Trenches.

At the outset no labour other than can be found by the Infantry Brigades themselves will be available for this work.

In the 5th Brigade area, it is considered that reopening the Grenadier Graben between Lille Road and the entrance to the Volker Tunnel in Black Line would be the quickest way of getting good communication.

In 6th and 13th Brigade areas attention must be devoted at first to the C.T.s on the forward slope of the ridge.   In view of the exposed nature of the ground, it will be difficult to dig now C.T.s and it will therefore be quicker to improve the existing C.T.s by putting in heavy traverses.

These forward C.T.s should be defended by Stokes Mortars posted in the vicinity of the observation line.

8. Action of Artillery.

Will be issued shortly as Appendix D.[1]

9. Action of Machine Guns.

See Appendix B and Tracing X attached.

10. Employment of Tanks.

(i)   No. 12 Company, D Bn. Heavy Branch M.G. Corps (with H.Q. in Bois de Maroeuil) has been detailed to assist this Division with two sections of four tanks each.

(ii)   The Southern Section will co-operate with the 6th Canadian Infantry Brigade and the Northern Section with the 13th British Brigade.

(iii)   The two Sections will be assembled under cover prior to Zero at a starting point in Elbe Trench between Rietz and Denis la Rocque.

(iv)   The two Sections will leave their starting point at Zero and advance to the Red Line which they are timed to reach at Zero plus four hours : the Southern Section advancing astride the Neuville—Thélus Road and the Northern Section astride Grenadier Graben.

(v)   The advance from the Red Line will be made in line with the Infantry, following immediately behind the barrage.

The Southern Section will send two Tanks round the Southern edge and two Tanks round the Northern edge, of Thélus.   As soon as the Village has been taken this Section will move to the vicinity of Thélus Wood and await orders.

The Northern Section will send two Tanks against point A.6.a.8.3, and two Tanks against point A.6.a.9½.9 (North corner

[1] Not reproduced.

of Counts Wood), in Thélus Trench : after crossing this trench each half section will advance astride one of the lines of wire and trench, running S.E. along Hill 140, as far as the Blue Line : thence the whole Section will rejoin the Southern Section near Thélus Wood and await orders.

The approximate lines of advance are shown in Map D.

(vi) The O.C. 12th Company will be at Divisional Report Centre. The O.C. Southern Section will be in Zivy Cave with G.O.C. 6th Brigade, and the O.C. Northern Section will be in Paynesley Report Centre with G.O.C. 13th Brigade.

(vii) Detailed instructions as regards assembly, routes and signals will be issued later.

11. **Employment of Field Companies & Pioneers.**

These Units will be employed under the orders of the C.R.E. as follows :—

(i) 6 Sections Field Companies for construction of Strong Points. (Vide Para. 7 (c) (vi) above.)

(ii) 2 Sections Field Companies for extension of Water Supply System.

(iii) 1 Section Field Company opening up Mule track to Lille Road.

(iv) 1 Company (3 Platoons) Pioneers burying cable Southern route.

(v) 1 Company (3 Platoons) Pioneers burying cable Northern route.

⎱ Vide Para. 17 (i) below.

(vi) 1 Company (3 Platoons) Pioneers extending Mowcop Spur of tramline towards Les Tilleuls.

(vii) 1 Company (3 Platoons) Pioneers opening up and repairing Neuville St. Vaast—Thélus Road.

Three Sections Field Companies and one Platoon per Company of Pioneers will be kept in Reserve at Mont St. Eloy for unforeseen contingencies.

Time and places at which the various parties are to assemble : instructions as to responsibility for sending them forward (vide Para. 7, Section IX, S.S.135) and the approximate route to be followed by the Mule Track will be notified later.

12. **Employment of Stokes Mortars.**

The fullest possible use of Stokes Mortars will be made during the operations in accordance with the principles laid down in S.S. 135, Sect. XX.

(i) Reference Para. 2, Sect. XX.).

(a) The Stokes Batteries of 4th and 5th Brigades will be employed on this work. Total—16 Mortars.

Each Battery will have its own Brigade front as its zone.

(b) Emplacements will be selected and prepared by Batteries concerned under the orders of G.O.sC. 4th and 5th Brigades.

(c) Targets will be points selected by G.O.sC. 4th and 5th Brigades in German front and support lines in their respective Zones.

(d) Duration of Bombardment.

On front line ; Zero to Zero plus one minute (Artillery lift at Zero plus three minutes)—on support line, Zero plus one

G

minute to Zero plus six minutes (Artillery lift at Zero plus eight minutes).

After Zero plus six minutes cease fire and prepare to advance.

(*e*)   Ammunition supply.

Six minutes' rapid fire at 30 rounds per mortar per minute—total 180 rounds per mortar for bombardment plus 120 rounds per mortar for emergencies vide Para. 2 (iv), Sect. XX.

Total to be dumped at each emplacement—300 rounds.

(ii)   Reference Para. 3, Sect. XX.

Instead of sending forward two mortars complete with each section, it is suggested that only one mortar with spare parts from the second mortar should be sent forward per section, the second mortar with its crew being withdrawn to some suitable dugout where they would remain available to replace casualties : the carriers allotted to the second mortar should accompany the mortar going forward.

(iii)   Reference Para. 4, Sect. XX.

As soon as the objective has been gained, the second mortar of each section should be sent up to join the other mortar in action, while the carriers would commence building up a dump of ammunition at the mortars, drawing from the nearest dump.

13. Communication Trenches & Trench Police.

(*a*)   Communication trenches are shown in Map A and in the special diagram already issued. IN Trenches are Blue, OUT Trenches are Red.

Another IN Trench (Macdonell Trench) shown on Map D has been constructed from Rietz Avenue to Paynesley. 3rd Canadian Division will have joint use of De la Fourche as an IN trench.

In that portion of Assembly Area of 13th Brigade in 3rd Canadian Division area, Chassery is an IN trench and Roy is an OUT trench.

(*b*)   Brigades holding the line will be responsible for detailing the necessary Trench Police to regulate the traffic. From 12 noon on Y day, each Brigade will be responsible for policing the IN and OUT trenches of their own Assembly Areas (with the exception of the IN and OUT trenches in that portion of the 3rd Canadian Division area allotted to the 13th Brigade for Assembly purposes).

The entrances and exits on the Bethune Road will be policed by Corps Cyclists forming part of the Battle Stragglers Posts under the orders of the A.P.M.

14. Assembly Areas.

These are shown on Map D and are allotted as follows :—

To 4th Brigade. 4th Bde. area as far West as Vistula (exclusive).

To 5th Brigade. 5th Bde. area as far West as Parallel VIII (exclusive).

To 6th Brigade. Remainder of Divisional area East of Béthune Road and South of Denis la Rocque (exclusive).

To 13th Brigade. Remainder of Divisional area together with that portion of the 3rd Canadian Division area coloured Green.

4th, 5th and 6th Brigades will each be responsible for constructing their own Assembly Trenches. 6th Brigade will be responsible for repairing Assembly Trenches for 13th Brigade : details to be arranged direct between Brigades concerned.

15. Headquarters. (See Map D.)

Divisional Headquarters.	Château d'Acq.
Divl. Report Centre.	Aux Rietz Cave.

4th Brigade.

Bde. Report Centre.	Zivy Cave.
Right Assaulting Bn.	Zivy Cave.
Left Assaulting Bn.	Dugout No. 7 near junction of Guillermot and Mill Street.
Reserve Bn.	Zivy Cave.
Mopping Up Bn.	Dugouts Nos. 1 & 2 in Guillermot about A.10.a.1.8.

5th Brigade.

Bde. Report Centre.	A.4.c.2.5½. In Paynesley trench 150 yds. S.E. of junction of this trench with Denis la Rocque.
Right Assaulting Bn.	Present Right Coy. H.Q. in O.61.
Left Assaulting Bn.	At junction of Denis la Rocque and O.61.
Reserve Bn.	With Left Assaulting Bn.
Mopping Up Bn.	Miner's dugout No. 1 near Sapper Road A.3.d.3.7.

6th Brigade.

Brigade Report Centre.	Zivy Cave.
Two Battalions.	Grenadier Post (Bois de Abris), A.9.a.4.0.
Two Battalions.	Advanced Bde. H.Q. on Territorial Trench A.8.d.6.3.

13th Brigade.

Brigade Report Centre.	With 5th Brigade Report Centre.
Two Battalions.	Miner's dugouts No. 2 near Sapper Road A.3.d.3.7.
Two Battalions.	Winchester House A.9.a.9.3.

16. Allotment of Headquarters after the Objective has been gained, vide Paras. 2 and 3, Sect. 13 of S.S. 135.

These are allotted as follows :—(See Maps A and D.)

(i)   Battalion of 4th Brigade detailed for Red objective—Ulmer signal dugout at A.11.a.¼.5½.

(ii)   Battalion of 5th Brigade detailed for Red objective—Volker Signal dugout in Volker Tunnel at A.4.d.9.9¾.

(iii)   6th Brigade Report Centre—Dugouts in Felsenkeller Weg about A.11.a.4.8½.

(iv)   13th Brigade Report Centre—as for (ii).

(v)   Battalions of 6th Brigade—Enemy Signal dugout at

A.5.d.½.0 (Les Tilleuls) and dugouts about A.5.d.3½.3 in Red line.

(vi)   Battalions of 13th Brigade—Cramer Signal dugout at A.5.b.7½.3¼ and dugouts in immediate vicinity, also Berlin Signal dugout at A.5.c.6.9 just North of Balloon Avenue.

These Report Centres and Headquarters should be occupied as soon as the situation permits.

17. Signal Communications.   (See Map A.)

(i) Buried Cable.

Prior to Zero two main routes will be pushed forward as far across No Man's Land as possible.   The Southern route from Zivy Cave through Zivy Subway to Phillip Crater.   The Northern route from 5th Brigade Report Centre by subway and mine galleries to Lichfield Crater.   As soon as the situation permits these cables will be pushed forward as follows :—

Southern route by Felsen Keller Weg to vicinity of Les Tilleuls passing Ulmer Signal dugout and position selected for 6th Brigade Advanced Report Centre.

Northern route via Volker Tunnel of Pioneers along Grenadier Graben to Cramer Signal dugout.   One Company will be employed to bury cable on each route.   The technical supervision of laying cable will be provided by 2nd Canadian Divisional Signal Company for the Southern route, and by the Canadian Corps Signal Company for the Northern route.

(ii) Visual.

The scheme for Visual signalling in connection with O.P.s has already been issued to all concerned under G.I.467 dated 24th February, 1917.

(iii) Power Buzzers.

Four power buzzers and two amplifiers are available for the Division.   These are allotted as follows :—

1 Buzzer to 4th Brigade to be sent forward as soon as possible to Ulmer Signal dugout.

1 Power buzzer to 5th Brigade to be sent forward as soon as possible to Volker Signal dugout.

1 Power buzzer to 6th Brigade to be sent forward to vicinity of Les Tilleuls.

1 Power buzzer to 13th Brigade to be sent forward to Cramer Signal dugout.

Brigades concerned will be responsible for providing personnel for working (three men) and carrying sets and for sending the buzzers forward as soon as the situation permits.

1 Amplifier will be located in the vicinity of Zivy Cave in telephonic communication with 4th and 6th Brigade Report Centres and the other amplifier in the vicinity of 5th Brigade Report Centre and in telephonic communication with 5th and 13th Brigade Report Centres.

These amplifiers will be worked by personnel supplied by and under the orders of the Corps Wireless Officer, the actual positions for them being selected by O.C. Divisional Signal Company in conjunction with the Corps Wireless Officer.

(iv) Pigeons.

Six pigeons per day are available for each Brigade and

will be distributed to Units as required by the Brigade Commander. These pigeons will " home " to Mont St. Eloy where the messages will be transmitted by wire to Divisional Report Centre and thence to Brigade Report Centres.

The allotment of birds will be delivered daily at a Forward Cage at Divisional Report Centre by motor cyclist.

Battalion Orderlies working under orders of Brigade Signal Sections will carry the birds from this cage to the Trench Stations.

(v) Despatch Riders.

One Troop Canadian Light Horse has been placed at the disposal of the Division and will be under the orders of the A.P.M. They will be used to supplement the motor cyclist despatch riders as required. O.C. 2nd Canadian Divisional Signal Coy. will indent on the A.P.M. for any men required.

18. Distinguishing Flags.   Reference Para. *a* (ii) Sect. III. S.S. 135.

Assaulting troops of 2nd Canadian Division and 13th Brigade will carry the Divisional Battle Flag, a yellow disc with a Black Maple Leaf centre ; two discs per platoon being carried.

The 1st Canadian Division are carrying a dark Blue and Yellow Flag and the 3rd Canadian Division a Black and Red Flag.

These discs and Flags must be waved and not stuck in the ground.

19. Instructions to Assaulting Troops.

The instructions contained in S.S. 135, Sects. XXVI, XXVII and XXVIII must be fully explained to all ranks taking part in the Assault.

20. Medical Arrangements.

A.D.M.S. has already issued instructions to all concerned.

21. Administrative Arrangements.

Instructions as to Water, Dumps, Tramlines, Battle Stragglers Posts, Prisoners of War, Salvage, Burial Parties, Forward Move of 1st Line Transport and Refitting will be issued by A.A. & Q.M.G.

N. W. Webber,
Lieut.-Colonel,
General Staff,
2nd Canadian Division.

G.H.Q. LETTER O.A.D. 350, 26TH MARCH 1917

To

General Sir H. S. Horne, K.C.B.,
  Commanding First Army.
General Sir H. C. O. Plumer, G.C.M.G., K.C.B.,
  Commanding Second Army.
General Sir E. H. H. Allenby, K.C.B.,
  Commanding Third Army.
General Sir H. S. Rawlinson, Bt., K.C.B., K.C.V.O.,
  Commanding Fourth Army.
General Sir H. de la P. Gough, K.C.B.,
  Commanding Fifth Army.
Lt.-General Sir C. T. McM. Kavanagh, K.C.B., C.V.O., D.S.O.,
  Commanding Cavalry Corps.

1. The enemy has withdrawn to the Hindenburg Line and the Cojeul switch,[1] leaving delaying detachments in front of that line.

There are indications that the enemy's intention may be to withdraw from the Arras—Vimy front to the Drocourt—Quéant line or, even if pressed, to the Marquion—Arleux—Douai [2] line. These indications are not sufficiently definite at present to warrant any definite conclusion on the subject.

2. The Fourth and Fifth Armies will continue to press the enemy's rearguards back to the Hindenburg Line and to get into touch with and reconnoitre that line as early as the resources placed at their disposal will permit.

A line of resistance will be established on the front Germaine—Beauvois—Poeuilly—Bernes—Marquaix—Longavesnes—Lieramont—Nurlu—Manancourt—Barastre—Mory. Subsequently a second line of resistance will be established further forward.

3. The Fifth Army will also prepare to deliver an attack on the Cojeul switch on the front Quéant—Ecoust, in conjunction with the operations of the Third Army, and will lend such assistance in

[1] For this title see p. 88. It was in effect the northern end of the Hindenburg Line.

[2] Air reconnaissances reported the existence of this line on the 17th and 18th March. On the 26th, three days after this letter was written, it was reported that it " did not exist " as a main line of defence, though there might be some short sections of trench.

artillery to the right of the Third Army attack as may be possible in view of the difficulties of bringing forward heavy and siege batteries.

The M.G.R.A., G.H.Q., will arrange for the co-ordination of the artillery between the Third and Fifth Armies.

4. If the enemy intends to withdraw it is important that he shall not be permitted to do so unmolested. Every endeavour is to be made to gain early information of his intentions by observation, raiding, and, if necessary, minor operations.

The First and Third Armies will be prepared to carry out at 24 hours' notice minor operations to penetrate and hold selected portions of the enemy's front line system in order to upset his arrangements and clear up the situation more definitely.

These Armies will also be prepared, by the 1st of April, or earlier if possible, to deliver a general assault, at 24 hours' notice, on the whole of the enemy's front system (on the Arras—Vimy front of attack) if it becomes clear that he is withdrawing ; and to follow up success gained in this assault.

The general infantry assault (full programme) is to be ready to be launched on the 8th April.

5. The Second Army will continue to push forward its preparations for the attack on the Messines—Wytschaetc Ridge. It will also make constant endeavours by all methods to ascertain the enemy's movements and intentions.

L. E. KIGGELL,
Lieut.-General,
Chief of the General Staff.

G.H.Q.,
23rd March, 1917.

BATTLES OF ARRAS

FIRST ARMY ORDER No. 101,
26TH MARCH 1917

1. (a) It is the intention of the Commander-in-Chief to attack the enemy with the Third and First Armies on a front from a point south-east of Arras to the Vimy Ridge inclusive.

(b) The task of the Third Army is to capture the enemy's trench systems on both banks of the River Scarpe, east of Arras, and to operate in the direction of Cambrai.

(c) The task of the First Army is to form a strong defensive flank for the operations of the Third Army by the capture of the Vimy Ridge from the Commandant's House to Gunner Crater, both inclusive ; and to exploit success by operating in the direction of Douai.

2. (a) The Army Commander intends to employ the Canadian Corps, reinforced by the 5th Division, and by certain heavy artillery of the I. Corps, to carry out the attack on the Vimy Ridge.

(b) XIII. Corps will be in Army Reserve, and will be available for further operations towards Douai ; together with any cavalry which may be attached to the Army.

(c) I. Corps and XI. Corps will hold the defensive front of the First Army.

(d) Portuguese Expeditionary Force will remain in Army Reserve and continue its training.

(e) II. Corps will be in the First Army area, and will be held in G.H.Q. reserve.

3.   The attack will be carried out on a day " Z " in accordance with the scheme already submitted by the Canadian Corps.

The infantry will assault at an hour Zero which will be communicated later.

The date of " Z " day has been communicated verbally to Corps Commanders.

4.   The G.O.C.R.A., First Army, will command the artillery of the Canadian Corps, and that portion of the I. Corps artillery which is to support the operation ; and will establish his advanced headquarters at the Advanced Headquarters of the Canadian Corps from 12 noon on 1st April.

5.   The artillery bombardment will be divided into a preparatory

period, which has already commenced, and the bombardment, which will commence on 2nd April.

6. Between 27th and 31st March, XI. Corps will carry out a demonstration, including a balloon concentration and artillery registration, on the Aubers Ridge front, in conjunction with similar action by the right flank corps of the Second Army. Detailed instructions have been issued separately.

7. The I. and XI. Corps, prior to " Z " day, will make every effort to deceive the enemy as to the exact limits of the operation ; and on " Z " day will occupy his attention with artillery, rifle and machine-gun fire.

8. If it appears probable that the enemy intends to withdraw at any time between now and " Z " day, the Canadian Corps will be prepared to penetrate and hold certain selected portions of the enemy's front line system at 24 hours' notice, in order to upset his arrangements, and clear up the situation more definitely.

Instructions for such action, and for co-operation with the left flank Corps of the Third Army, have been issued separately.

9. If it becomes clear that the enemy is withdrawing, the Canadian Corps will be prepared to assault and capture the enemy's front line system of trenches up to and including the Black Line in the Canadian Corps scheme, at 24 hours' notice, on or after 1st April.

10. Advanced First Army Headquarters will be established at Ranchicourt at 12 noon on April 4th.

W. H. ANDERSON,
Major-General,
Issued at 11 A.M.   General Staff, First Army.

BATTLES OF ARRAS

VII. CORPS INSTRUCTIONS, G.C.R. 604/183, 26TH MARCH 1917

In continuation of previous instructions under this file :—

1.   The general plan of operations, as far as it affects the VII. Corps, is as follows :—
      The Third Army will break through the enemy's defences on the front from Mercatel northwards, simultaneously with an attack on the Vimy Ridge by the First Army.   This is the first operation, and will be carried out by the three corps now holding the Third Army front.   As soon as this operation is accomplished, the advance will be taken up by the Cavalry Corps and the XVIII. Corps, passing through the front of the VI. Corps on our left.

2.   The task of the VII. Corps has already been defined.   The effect of the enemy's recent withdrawal on the VII. Corps share in the main operation has been to change our task from an attack in a south-easterly direction from prepared positions, to an attack in an easterly and north-easterly direction from improvised positions.   But the objects of our attack remain the same : that is, to break the enemy's defensive line on the right of the Third Army front, to over-run all his defences as far as the Green Line, and to clear and hold the southern flank of the gap which the VI. Corps, advancing simultaneously with us, will have made.

3.   A new and final map, which cancels those previously issued, is attached ; on it are shown the dividing lines between divisions, their successive objectives, and the scope of their tasks.   The dividing line with the VI. Corps has been altered by the Army, and Wancourt is now included in the final objective of the 30th Division.

4.   To take the tasks allotted to divisions in detail :—
      (a) Only the extreme point of the 14th Division reaches the Brown Line.   From the Blue to the Brown Lines there are few trenches or obstacles in the 14th Division's path, but troops must be pushed forward in accordance with the time table to clear the ground and to keep touch between the VI. Corps on the left and the 56th Division on the right.   As soon as its leading troops reach the Brown Line, the task of the 14th Division is done.

(*b*) Similarly the Brown Line is the limit of the 56th Division's advance. It is essential however that, in accordance with the principle already laid down, the right of the 56th Division during the advance from the Blue to the Brown Line should have a reserve of strength, so that there may be troops available on that flank to assist the advance of the 30th Division by taking the trenches included in the latter's objective in flank and reverse.

(*c*) The 30th Division will push through to the Green Line, which will be consolidated. On leaving the Brown Line the 30th Division will extend its left so as to get into touch with the troops of the VI. Corps on the left. The 30th Division also must be prepared to assist the advance of the 21st Division by taking in flank and reverse the trenches on the latter's front.

(*d*) The 21st Division will conform to the advance of the 30th Division and eventually establish itself on the Green Line.

The right of the 21st Division will stand fast, as will also the troops of the V Corps (Fifth Army) on the immediate right. The point of junction between the 21st Division and the V. Corps will be fixed as the result of the developments of the next few days.

It is probable that the Fifth Army will attack further to the east, but there will be a non-attacking front of some 5,000 yards on the immediate right of the 21st Division's attack.

5. As soon as the advance from the Brown Line has started the 14th and 56th Divisions will reform on the ground which they occupy. It is unlikely that the flow of fresh troops from behind will permit of these divisions being moved within 24 hours of Zero hour at least.

On reaching the Green Line, the 30th and 21st Divisions will hold such of their troops as are not required for consolidation in readiness to move further forward if required. These divisions may be called upon to relieve the Cavalry about Chérisy in the course of the night.

6. It is calculated that the VI. Corps will reach their Black Line at Zero plus 36 minutes.

The advance from the Black to the Blue Line is calculated to take 44 minutes. The Blue Line should therefore be reached at Zero plus 2 hours 44 minutes.

Leaving the Blue Line at Zero plus 6 hours 40 minutes, the Brown Line should be reached at Zero plus 8 hours.

The advance from the Brown Line will take place at Zero plus 10 hours, the Green Line being reached at Zero plus 12 hours.

7. Acknowledge.

J. BURNETT-STUART,
Brigadier-General,
General Staff, VII. Corps.

BATTLES OF ARRAS

CONSIDERATIONS OF PROBABLE ACTION AFTER THE ATTACK ON THE VIMY RIDGE, FIRST ARMY, No. G.S. 529 (*a*), 28TH MARCH 1917

Reference :—1/40,000 map.

1. Our troops on the evening of the battle.

Assuming success on the Vimy Ridge, the situation in the evening of 8th April [postponed 24 hours] may be as follows :—

> 1st Canadian Division—with its right on Farbus Wood ; and with 3 brigades, all of which have been employed.
>
> 2nd Canadian Division— about Bois Goulot and Thélus ; 3 brigades and a brigade of 5th Division attached, all of which have been employed.
>
> 3rd Canadian Division—about Folie Farm and the Folie Wood ; with 2 brigades which have been employed and possibly one fresh brigade.
>
> 4th Canadian Division—south of Givenchy, with probably one fresh brigade.
>
> 5th Division—with 2 fresh brigades.
>
> XIII. Corps—concentrated on a front of one division ; head of leading division about Estrée-Cauchie and Gouy ; ready to move on Neuville St. Vaast.
>
> A Cavalry Division—about Frévin Capelle, in the area of Third Army.
>
> XVII. Corps, Third Army—with its left on Farbus Wood, through Maison de la Côte (B.20.d.6.2) and Point du Jour to the Scarpe.

2. Nature of retreat of the enemy.

The enemy will either be in a position to retire methodically, occupying his prepared positions east of the Vimy Ridge, or he may be driven back in confusion.

3. Action by enemy in case of methodical withdrawal.

Taking the first case. The enemy will not have been driven from Givenchy or the Pimple, and he will almost certainly hold on to those and to his line joining Givenchy to Vimy. He may hold the line of the railway, and Willerval and Bailleul ; or he may go back to the Gavrelle—Oppy—Arleux-en-Gohelle line, holding thence via Willerval to Vimy and so connecting to his original line about Givenchy.

The Gavrelle—Oppy—Méricourt line is wired, and the enemy seem certain to defend it, if only to gain time to readjust their line to the north. An immediate withdrawal behind the Gavrelle—Méricourt line would make their commanders nervous of the guns and troops in the coal area Givenchy-en-Gohelle—Liévin—Lens.

4. Our action.

When our heavy guns are brought up on the Vimy Ridge they will be within range of the Gavrelle—Oppy—Arleux-en-Gohelle part of their line ; it will be necessary to get field guns into the folds of the ground west of Willerval ; and our action will be on the following lines :—

Canadian Corps—to attack the Pimple and occupy Vimy and Willerval, and subsequently send on Corps Mounted Troops on Carriéres du Mt. Foret and Acheville, with the object of securing tactical points till infantry advanced guards come up, so as to hold a defensive flank along the Vimy—Rouvroy road, facing north. 5th Division to be first employed in the advance east, so as to be available for transfer to XIII. Corps when tactical considerations render it desirable.

XIII. Corps—to obtain possession of Bailleul, operating thence on Gavrelle—Oppy—Arleux-en-Gohelle ; using the Roclincourt—Bailleul—Oppy ; and Bailleul—Gavrelle roads.

5. Further advance.

Having occupied the Gavrelle—Oppy—Acheville line, the next step is to the Quéant—Drocourt line, which the enemy must hold if he has still got his troops in the Lens—Liévin salient. This line is also wired, and the opportunity of using a large body of cavalry does not seem to have arrived until the enemy is known to have vacated this line.

Canadian Corps would continue to hold a defensive flank facing north along the Vimy—Bois Bernard ridge, its right keeping touch with the left of XIII. Corps, to which the 5th Division will have been transferred.

XIII. Corps would advance on Vitry-en-Artois — Izel-les-Equerchin—Drocourt.

6. Action by enemy and our troops in case of rapid withdrawal of enemy.

If the attack on the Arras—Vimy front is so successful that the enemy withdrew without being able to hold the villages east of the ridge (Vimy—Willerval—Bailleul) or the Gavrelle—Oppy—Arleux-en-Gohelle line, an opportunity for the employment of cavalry would arise which would enable the Army Commander to employ the 1st Cavalry Division to push forward on to the line Douai—Hénin Liétard, and secure the railway at Hénin Liétard and the locks and bridges on the Sensée and Haute Deule Canals between Corbehem—Vitry-en-Artois (junction of Scarpe and Sensée) and the Pont à Sault (N.E. of Dourges) with the object of preventing destruction of bridges and inundations.

This advance would be supported by the XIII. Corps moving forward on the following roads :—

(a) Gavrelle—Brebières—Douai road.
(b) Oppy—Izel—Esquerchin road.

The action of the Canadian Corps would be similar to the first case, viz.—to seize Vimy and form a defensive flank facing north, on the general line Vimy—Carriéres du Mt. Foret—Acheville.

W. H. ANDERSON,
Major-General,
General Staff, First Army.

BATTLES OF ARRAS

THIRD ARMY ORDER No. 173,
1ST APRIL 1917

1.   The enemy has fallen back to the Hindenburg Line and holds some advanced positions south and west of it.
Four German Divisions hold the front from Croisilles to Roclincourt.

2.   The Fourth and Fifth Armies are facing the enemy on the Hindenburg Line.   The Fifth Army holds the front Beaumetz lez Cambrai—Croisilles.   The Fifth Army is to attack east and west of Bullecourt on a date subsequent to " Z ".
The First Army is to capture the Vimy Ridge simultaneously with the attack of the Third Army and is to secure the front Commandant's House (one mile S.E. of Thélus) to Givenchy.

3.   The Third Army will break through the enemy's defences on the front Croisilles, Commandant's House (one mile S.E. of Thélus).   The Third Army will then capture the German defensive line which runs from Arras to Cambrai (the Hindenburg Line) by attacking it in flank and rear, and will advance on Cambrai.

4.   The bombardment of the enemy's defences will be carried out during V, W, X and Y days.

5.   The operation of breaking through the enemy's defences will be carried out by the VII., VI., and XVII. Corps :—

VII. Corps—14th, 30th, 56th and 21st Divisions.
VI. Corps— 3rd, 12th, 15th and 37th Divisions.
XVII. Corps— 9th, 34th, 51st and 4th Divisions.

6.   (a) Corps will assault the enemy's front line system simultaneously at Zero hour and will gain the Black Line at Zero plus 36 minutes.
(b) Corps will advance from the Black Line at Zero plus 2 hours and assault the enemy's second line system, reaching the Blue Line between Zero plus 2 hours and 44 minutes and Zero plus 3 hours.
(c) Corps will advance from the Blue Line at Zero plus 6 hours 40 minutes and will reach the Brown Line at Zero plus 8 hours.
(d) Corps will advance from the Brown Line at Zero plus 10 hours and will reach the Green Line at Zero plus 12 hours.

7.   During the operations up to the Green Line certain situations may be presented with which it is intended to deal as follows :—

(i) The enemy may be disorganized and in retreat.

In this case the enemy would probably endeavour to hold the Quéant—Drocourt Line and reorganize behind it.

Our action will be to follow the enemy quickly and gain this line at the same time as his retreating troops.

For this purpose, the Cavalry Corps (2nd and 3rd Cavalry Divisions and 17th Infantry Division) will pass the Green Line and pursue. The Cavalry Corps will be supported by such Divisions of the VII., VI., and XVII. Corps as are available, or, if none are available, by Divisions drawn from the XVIII. Corps and placed under the Command of the VII., VI., and XVII. Corps as required.

(ii) The enemy may bring up his reserves and show a strong battle front about the Green Line or in front of it.

In this case the Cavalry Corps will not advance.

The VII., VI., and XVII. Corps will continue the attack and may if necessary be reinforced by Divisions drawn from the XVIII. Corps and by the Infantry Division of the Cavalry Corps.

L. J. Bols,
Major-General,
General Staff, Third Army.

Issued at 2 p.m.

BATTLES OF ARRAS

CAVALRY CORPS INSTRUCTIONS, G.X. 96/48, 1ST APRIL 1917

Forwarded herewith " Instructions issued to the Cavalry Corps for the Offensive Operations to be carried out by the Third Army ". Please acknowledge by wire.

A. F. HOME,
B.G.G.S.

Cavalry Corps.

Secret.

INSTRUCTIONS ISSUED TO THE CAVALRY CORPS FOR THE OFFENSIVE OPERATIONS TO BE CARRIED OUT BY THE THIRD ARMY

1.   The general intention of the operations is to drive the German Armies out of France and Belgium.

2.   The general plan for the offensive consists of the following operations :—

   (*a*)   The First Army is to capture the Vimy Ridge simultaneously with the attack of the Third Army, and secure the front Commandant's House (one mile S.E. of Thélus) to Givenchy.
   The Third Army will break through the enemy's defences on the front Mercatel, Commandant's House (one mile S.E. of Thélus). The Third Army will then capture the German defensive line which runs from Arras to Cambrai (the Hindenburg Line) by attacking it in flank and rear, and will continue to operate towards Cambrai.

   (*b*)   At a date which will be notified later the Fifth Army will deliver an attack on the Hindenburg Line from the direction of Quéant with the object of breaking the enemy line opposite that place.

   (*c*)   The attacks mentioned above will have the further purpose of drawing the enemy reserves, so as to help an attack by the French Armies with large effectives with the purpose of breaking the enemy line.

3.   The operations which affect the Cavalry Corps are those mentioned in para. 2 (*a*) and (*b*). The Cavalry Corps (less the 1st and 5th Cavalry Divisions) will come under the command of the Third Army. The 4th Cavalry Division will join the Cavalry Corps

H

from the Fifth Army as laid down later.   The 1st Cavalry Division
will be under the orders of the First Army.[1]   The 5th Cavalry
Division will be under the orders of G.H.Q.

4.   The order of battle of the Third Army will be as follows :—

VII. Corps	.	5 Divisions.
VI. Corps	.	4 Divisions.
XVII. Corps	.	4 Divisions.
In Army Reserve XVIII. Corps	.	4 Divisions.
Cavalry Corps	.	Consisting of 2nd, 3rd, and 4th Cavalry Divisions and 17th Infantry Division. (The artillery of this division will be attached to XVII. Corps, but will rejoin the division as soon as it moves.)

5.   The preparatory positions of all troops before Zero are shewn
in Appendix " A ".
     The boundaries between the Corps, and the objectives of the
Corps, are shewn in Appendix " B ".[2]

6.   The attack on Z day may be divided into four phases, the phase
being shown by the Black, Blue, Brown and Green lines in Appendix
" B ".
     First Phase.
     The attack will start at Zero and will have for its objective
the enemy's front line system up to the Black line on the map.   It
is estimated that the Black line will be reached at Z +36 minutes.
In order to bring up fresh troops, and to prepare for a further advance,
a pause will be made on the Black line till Z +2 hours.
     Second Phase.
     The attack from the Black line will start at Z +2 hours, and
will have for its objective the enemy's second line system up to the
Blue line.   It is estimated that the Blue line will be reached at
Z +2 hours 44 minutes.   In order to move forward artillery and
bring up fresh troops, a pause will be made on the Blue line till
Z +6 hours and 40 minutes.
     Third Phase.
     The attack from the Blue line will start at Z +6 hours and
40 minutes, and will have for its objective the Brown line.   It is
estimated that the Brown line will be reached in 1 to 2 hours, and
taking the latter estimate, would bring the time to Z +8 hours.
After the capture of the Green line the VI. Corps will form a defensive
flank facing north, from the right of the XVII. Corps about Fampoux
to l'Ecluse, maintaining touch with the Cavalry Corps or the XVIII.
Corps.

7.   The Mission of the Cavalry Corps.
     The mission of the Cavalry Corps is to seize and hold the line
Riencourt—Cagnicourt—Dury—Etaing, with a view to further
operations towards Cambrai.

     [1] See amendment dated the 5th April placing the First Cavalry Division
in G.H.Q. reserve.
     [2] Neither of these appendices is reproduced.

This object may be attained in two ways :—

(*a*)   On Z day by an advance through Arras, in which case the 2nd and 3rd Cavalry Divisions will move astride the main Arras—Cambrai road, followed by the 17th (Infantry) Division. The 4th Cavalry Division will come into reserve about Croisilles.

(*b*)   At a later date by an advance through the Fifth Army front, in which case the 4th Cavalry Division followed by the 2nd Cavalry Division, will advance through the gap that is made, the 3rd Cavalry Division coming into reserve about Croisilles.   The 17th (Infantry) Division would join the Cavalry by the main Arras—Cambrai road as soon as the situation permitted.

8.   The routes through Arras, the alternate routes north and south of Arras, and the Cavalry tracks across our trench system, are shewn in the map, Appendix " C ".[1]

Route " A " is allotted to the 3rd Cavalry Division.

„ " C "
„ " D " } are allotted to the 2nd Cavalry Division.

9.   (*a*)   In the event of an advance through Arras, the 2nd and 3rd Cavalry Divisions will move to positions of readiness as follows :—

In accordance with the situation of the moment, Cavalry Corps will issue orders so that the Divisions will be placed in the following positions :—

3rd Cavalry Division.   Head at G.13.d.9.4.[2]   Sheet 51.B. 1/40,000.   Remainder of the division echeloned along the Wanquentin—Duisans—main St. Pol—Arras road.

2nd Cavalry Division.   Head at G.34.a.9.1.[3]   Sheet 51.B. 1/40,000.   Remainder of the division echeloned along the Wailly—Crinchon Valley road.

17th Infantry Division.   Preparing to be ready to advance. Two Brigades via Agnez-les-Duisans, Duisans, and the main St. Pol—Arras road, one Brigade via Dainville to follow the 3rd and 2nd Cavalry Divisions respectively.

(*b*)   The move forward to the final position of readiness will again take place under orders to be issued by Cavalry Corps. The order to advance through and round Arras will be issued with a view to bringing the leading Cavalry Divisions into the following positions of readiness by the time the infantry attacks are expected to reach the Brown line.

3rd Cavalry Division.   Head on cavalry track at eastern end of H.31.b.[4]   Sheet 51.B.   N.W.   1/20,000, and remainder echeloned along Route " A ".

2nd Cavalry Division.   Head on cavalry track at eastern end of M.6.b. and d.[5]   Sheet 51.B.   S.W.   1/20,000 remainder echeloned along route " C " or " D ".

17th Infantry Division.   Will move in two columns along

---

[1] Not reproduced.
[2] At the Faubourg de Baudimont, north-west of Arras.
[3] At the Faubourg Ronville, south of Arras Station.
[4] North of Tilloy-lez-Mofflaines.
[5] South-west of Tilloy-lez-Mofflaines.

Routes " B " and " C " on receipt of orders from Corps Headquarters.

10.   The objectives of the Cavalry Divisions are as follows :—

(a)   1st Objective.   The line of the Sensée River from Fontaine-lez-Croisilles exclusive, to Vis-en-Artois and thence to Boiry-Notre Dame inclusive.

(b)   As soon as the Cavalry Corps is relieved by infantry (which may be infantry of the VI. and VII. Corps or of the XVIII. Corps), the second objective will be the line Riencourt—Cagnicourt—Dury—Etaing.

11.   In consequence, as soon as the infantry attacks have reached the high ground N.W. of Héninel, and that of Monchy-le-Preux, the cavalry will move forward to its first objective.

(a)   1st Objective.   The 2nd Cavalry Division (moving forward along the track it has prepared) will take and hold the high ground on the right bank of the River Sensée between Fontaine-lez-Croisilles and Vis-en-Artois, both exclusive.   It will cover its right flank on the general line Wancourt—Fontaine-lez-Croisilles.   The main Arras—Cambrai road will be exclusive to this Division.   The Zone of reconnaissance will be south and exclusive of the Arras—Cambrai road as far as La Brioche Fme, and from there along the line Sauchy Lestrée, Hayne-court, Ramillies, all exclusive.[1]

The 3rd Cavalry Division will take and hold the line Vis-en-Artois—Boiry-Notre Dame both inclusive.   The main Arras—Cambrai road is allotted to this division, but will not be available west of Les Fosses Fme N.11.b. sheet 51.B.S.W. 1/20,000. The Zone of reconnaissance will be north and inclusive of the Arras—Cambrai road as far as La Brioche Fme and from there along the line Sauchy Lestrée, Haynecourt, Ramillies, all inclusive.

The 17th Infantry Division will follow the 2nd and 3rd Cavalry Divisions closely.

Two brigades will move along " B " route.

One brigade will move along " C " route in rear of the 2nd Cavalry Division.

These moves will be made with a view to placing two brigades on the main Cambrai road, and one brigade on the Tilloy-lez-Mofflaines—Wancourt—Chérisy road, so as to be in a position to take over the 1st objective from the 2nd and 3rd Cavalry Divisions if required.

(b)   Aeroplane reports show that the so-called Quéant—Dury—Vitry-en-Artois line does not exist as a trench system south of Dury.   The situation may therefore arise that this position is not held by the enemy, and that the enemy, finding the Hindenburg Line turned, may retire faster than is anticipated, and in some disorder.   Should such a situation occur the Cavalry Corps must be ready to follow up the enemy at once. On reaching the first objective, strong reconnaissance detachments must be pushed forward at once to the 2nd objective to

[1] A line roughly 12 miles north of the Arras—Cambrai road.   See Map 1.   (Compiler's note.)

seize and hold the tactical points along it with a view to a rapid advance by the divisions to that objective.

Should time, daylight, and the enemy allow such a movement, the following situation might be produced by dark on Z day :—

The 2nd Cavalry Division holding the line Riencourt exclusive, to the main Arras—Cambrai road (exclusive) due south of Dury, with strong reconnoitring detachments sent forward to the line of the Canal.

The 3rd Cavalry Division continuing the line to Etaing, with strong reconnoitring detachments sent forward to the line of the Canal.

The 17th Division following the cavalry advance, and prepared to advance along :—

> (*a*) Chérisy—Cagnicourt road.
> (*b*) Main Cambrai road.
> (*c*) Boiry-Notre Dame—Dury road.

Should the above situation not arise, the advance to the second objective will take place as soon as the infantry of the VI. and VII. or XVIII. Corps relieve the Cavalry Corps, the objectives of the 3rd and 2nd Cavalry Divisions being as given above.

In all probability the 4th Cavalry Division will, in each case, come into reserve about Croisilles.

12. The further advance will be dictated by the situation. The general line of the advance will probably be north of Cambrai, between that place and the Sensée and L'Escaut Canals. The dividing line between division running from La Brioche Fme— Sauchy Lestrée—Haynecourt—Ramillies, all inclusive to the 3rd Cavalry Division.

13. Flares.

Cavalry Corps (except the 17th Infantry Division) will use the green flare at all times. Owing to the difficulty of replenishing supplies of these flares, the use of flares must be supervised by squadron and troop officers. Attention is called to Appendix " B ", para. 4.A.(i), " Instructions for the training of divisions for offensive action ". Cavalry Corps will lay down in orders at what places and at what times flares are to be lit. They will also be used as laid down in para. 4.A.(ii) in the above appendix. The 17th Infantry Division will use the red flares ordered for the infantry by the Fifth Army.

14. Maps.

(*a*) The 1/40,000 squared map will be used as long as the operations are confined to

> Sheet 51.B. and 51.C.
> Sheet 36.C.
> Sheet 57.C.

(*b*) The 1/20,000 trench map 51.B.N.W. and 51.B.S.W., 51.B.N.E. and 51.B.S.E. will be used for work in the trench area.

(*c*) At all other times 1/100,000 maps will be used except for communication with aeroplanes when the 1/40,000 squared map will be carried by such units as that have wireless with them.

(*d*) Whenever pin point references are made in any message or order they will be taken from the 1/40,000 or 1/20,000 map as far as issued. The sheet always will be quoted but not the scale of the map.

15. Dismounted Personnel.

Only such dismounted personnel as is necessary will be employed by divisions on the work in para. 9.

Each dismounted party will be under the command of a responsible officer.

16. The A.D. Signals will arrange to have communication with Tilloy-lez-Mofflaines and Croisilles as soon as possible after the infantry advance. As soon as the cavalry advance begins, the Corps Signals will establish an advanced post at either place, as may be ordered, and will be responsible for forwarding messages received there to Corps Headquarters.

17. Cavalry Corps Headquarters will be at Duisans, and the first move forward will be to Tilloy-lez-Mofflaines or Croisilles as circumstances direct."

Cavalry Corps,
G.X. 96/88.

With reference to " Instructions issued to the Cavalry Corps for the offensive operations to be carried out by Third Army ", No. G.X. 96/48, the following amendment is made to para. 3, line 5, reference to the 1st Cavalry Division :—

For " 1st Cavalry Division will be under the orders of the 1st Army "

Substitute

" The 1st Cavalry Division will be administered by the Cavalry Corps Headquarters, but will be held in G.H.Q. reserve."

2. In view of the above amendment, the rôle of the 1st Cavalry Division is a dual one ; it may be used under orders issued by G.H.Q. either :—

(*a*) To reinforce the Cavalry Corps east of Arras, or

(*b*) To reinforce the 1st Army in order to exploit a success north of the Scarpe.

3. The 1st Cavalry Division will therefore continue to keep close touch with the First Army, the dismounted men employed with the Canadian Corps will remain as already arranged. Secondly, it will keep in close touch with the 3rd Cavalry Division and the arrangements made by that division for a move forward to the east of Arras.

A. F. Home,
B.G.G.S.

Cavalry Corps,
5th April, 1917.

BATTLES OF ARRAS

XVII. CORPS ORDER No. 27,
2ND APRIL 1917

1.   The enemy opposite the Fifth Army and opposite the right of the Third Army has fallen back to the Hindenburg Line.

2.   The Third Army is ordered to break through the enemy's defences on the front Croisilles—Commandant's House (one mile south-east of Thélus), to capture the Hindenburg Line by attacking it in flank and rear, and to advance on Cambrai. The Canadian Corps is to deliver a simultaneous attack with a view to capturing the Vimy Ridge northwards from Commandant's House.

3.   The XVII. Corps will attack on the front between the R. Scarpe (exclusive) and the Arras—Lille road (inclusive) with the object of capturing the German 3rd trench system which runs through Athies, le Point du Jour, and Maison de la Côte, and of pushing on to the capture of Fampoux and the German 4th trench system as far north as Hyderabad Redoubt (inclusive).

4.   The attack will be carried out in accordance with the instructions given in XVII. Corps G.S. 32, dated 20th January 1917. The order of the assaulting divisions from right to left will be :—

        9th Division.
        34th Division.
        51st Division.

5.   The 4th Division will be in Corps Reserve and will be prepared to push through the 9th Division after the latter has captured the German 3rd trench system. Its task will be the capture of Fampoux and the German 4th trench system.

    Definite orders for this move will be given by the Corps.

6.   During the operations up to the Green line (see G.S. 32), certain situations may be presented with which it is intended to deal as follows :—

(i)   The enemy may be disorganized and in retreat. In this case he would probably try to hold the Quéant—Drocourt Line and reorganize behind it. Our action will be to follow the enemy quickly and gain this line at the same time as his retreating troops. For this purpose the Cavalry Corps will pass the Green line and pursue ; it will be supported by such divisions of the

VI., VII., and XVII. Corps as may be available or may be added to them for the purpose.

(ii) The enemy may bring up his reserves and show a strong battle front about the Green line or in front of it. In this case the Cavalry Corps will not advance, but the VI., VII., and XVII. Corps will continue the attack, reinforced if necessary by divisions of the XVIII. Corps.

7.   The hour of the assault—Zero—will be communicated later.

8.   Reports to Aubigny.

J. R. E. CHARLES,

Issued to Signals   Br.-General,
at 11 P.M.   General Staff.

BATTLES OF ARRAS

CAVALRY CORPS, MEANS OF COMMUNICATION, G.X. 96/48/1, 2ND APRIL 1917

Reference Cavalry Corps G.X. 96/48 of 1st April 1917,
" Instructions issued to the Cavalry Corps for Offensive
Operations ".

1.　　Small red and white flags will be carried by cavalry regiments, on the scale of one per troop, to denote positions of advanced detachments.

2.　　Appendix " C ", map shewing tracks over trench system, is forwarded herewith.[1] Track " A " will be marked by light blue and dark blue flags ; track " C " by blue and yellow flags.

3.　　Appendix " E " is forwarded herewith.

A. F. HOME,
B.G.G.S.

Cavalry Corps.

Appendix E.

1.　　The technical notes as regards the system and method of communications have been issued by the A.D. Signals Cavalry Corps to all concerned.

2.　　The means of communication at the disposal of the Cavalry Corps are :—
　　(a) Telegraph and telephone.
　　(b) Wireless.
　　(c) Despatch riders (cycle, horse and motor cycle).
　　(d) Pigeons.
　　(e) Visual signalling between units and to the kite balloon.

3.　　By Z day the following circuits will be installed.
　　(a) All divisions will be connected by telegraph and telephone to Corps Headquarters direct.
　　(b) The following means of communication forward will exist as below :—
　　　　(i)　　A route reconnoitred for terminal cables at

---

[1] Not reproduced.

G.17.d.41 Sheet 51 (*b*) N.W. in case of operations North of the Scarpe.

(ii)   Terminal cables at G.30.c.32 Sheet 51 (*b*) N.W. in case of operations due East from Arras.

(iii)   Terminal wire about B.3 Central Sheet 57 (*c*) 1/40,000 in case of operations North from the area Quéant—Croisilles.

(*c*) Arrangements have been made for pigeons to be issued to the divisions.

(*d*) The kite balloon (grey with black belts) will be ready to ascend at M.9.a.43 Sheet 51 (*b*) S.W. By night the balloon will notify that it is up ready to receive messages by firing the Very light signals already issued.

4.   All messages sent by wireless will be either by the B.A.B Code or in cipher. The 17th Division will use an address code which will be issued to all concerned. A code for the use of aeroplanes is laid down in " Instructions for the Training of Divisions for offensive Action " with the addition allowed by Cavalry Corps. The above instructions are not to be departed from and no other code is to be used.

5.   In the event of an advance, the importance of the despatch rider both horse and cycle must not be lost sight of. Cavalry Corps Headquarters will only be able to dispose of 1 weak troop to assist in a forward direction. Whenever possible a forward post will be established by Corps Headquarters and its position will be given in orders.

6.   All units must remember that a great strain will be thrown on the signal service and that the wires and wireless and kite balloon must be used for operations only. From Z day onwards divisions will arrange a post so that all other messages and letters will reach Corps Headquarters about 7 P.M. daily. Corps Headquarters will arrange a post which will reach divisions daily at the same time as orders.

7.   Routine situation reports will be sent by divisions to reach Cavalry Corps Headquarters at 6 A.M., 12 noon, 8 P.M. It is the duty of the signals to ask for these messages so that they may be sent off in time.

TELEGRAPHIC ORDERS BY FIFTH ARMY

0.0.49.   2/4/17.

Preparations for the attack on the Hindenburg Line must now be taken in hand with the greatest energy.   Every available heavy gun must be pushed up without further delay and got into action at suitable range.   All risks must be accepted.   Infantry must work forward to assaulting positions and any necessary trenches must be prepared.   Add'sd V. and I. Anzac Corps, rep't'd G.O.C.R.A., Q., C.E., D.D. Signals.

Fifth Army.   .   3 P.M.

BATTLES OF ARRAS

37TH DIVISION INSTRUCTIONS No. 6, ADMINISTRATIVE ARRANGEMENTS (Q), 2ND APRIL 1917

I.   Ammunition and Tools.

(a) Grenades, tools, etc. for fighting equipment are being collected at a provisional dump at Agnez-Duisans. At a date to be notified later all these stores will be sent to points on the line of march, or to areas to be occupied by brigades on X/Y night, at the discretion of brigade commanders, where grenades will be prepared under brigade arrangements and all stores laid out for distribution to units.

(b) Light T.M. ammunition, grenades, flares, etc. will, in the initial stages, be obtained from 3rd, 12th, and 15th divisional dumps east of Arras, vide Map D, issued with 37th Divisional Instructions No. 2.—112th Infantry Brigade drawing from 3rd Division ; 111th from 15th Division ; 63rd from 12th Division ; subsequently they will be obtained under divisional arrangements from corps dumps, and will be sent up to and distributed from an advanced divisional dump.

(c) To prevent any chance of sending grenades which have not been prepared forward to advanced dumps, each box will be marked as soon as the grenades are fuzed. The mark will be a notch cut with a knife in the centre of the hinged edge of the lid of the box, deep enough to be felt when handled in the dark.

II.   Supplies.

A.   To avoid confusion, the iron rations carried on the man normally for emergencies will be designated the " Emergency Iron Ration ".

B. (a) Normal supply trains will arrive up to Z +1 day[1] inclusive, but cannot be counted upon on Z and Z +1 days.

(b) Wheeled traffic will probably not be permitted to pass through Arras from Z +18 to Z +48 hours.

(c) To meet this situation :—

    (i) For men :

       One iron ration in addition to the emergency iron

---

[1] This is probably an error for Z minus 1 day.

ration will be issued to all ranks who are intended to pass through Arras on Z day.

These rations are now at a dump at Agnez-Duisans (K.11.d.1.1) and will be issued to infantry brigades etc. either direct from the dump to units or deposited in the equipping dumps on the line of march at the discretion of brigade commanders.

Men will therefore be fully rationed up to Z +1 day inclusive, on entering Arras, without taking the emergency iron ration into account.

Two additional iron rations per man have been dumped at a divisional dump on Blangy road, E. of Arras (G.23.a.3.2). These will be drawn on nights of Z and Z +1 days for consumption on Z +2 and Z +3 days respectively.

It is assumed that rations for consumption on Z +4 day will be available E. of Arras on Z +3 day and will be issued during the night of Z +3/Z +4 day under the normal system. This day's ration will be the one drawn from railhead on Y day and kept with divisional train until it can be delivered to first line transport.

(ii) 3 days' oats rations must be carried for every animal which is intended to go through Arras, with exception of animals earmarked for pack (which will only carry the unexpended portion) as their 3 days' are dumped now E. of Arras (G.23.a.3.2). As much hay as possible to be carried in nets or on vehicles. Hay for pack animals will be dumped at G.23.a.3.2 beforehand.

III.   Water.

A.   Refilling points.

   1.   Water lorries and water carts.

     (*a*) L.11.a.0.9 (water carts only).

     (*b*) L.18.d (on main road 1½ miles W. of Baudimont Gate).

     (*c*) Wells at (1) L.24.d (just S. of Racecourse).
                     (2) G.20.d (S. of Rifle Range).

     (*d*) G.21.b (Rue de St. Maurice, Arras).

     (*e*) G.23.c (Rue des Rosatis, Arras).

     (*f*) G.28.d (Rue de la République, Arras).

   2.   Water bottles.

     (*a*) L.18.d (on main road as in 1).

     (*b*) G.29.c.6.5 (Arras).

     (*c*) G.29.d (Rue des Trois Eglises, Arras).

     (*d*) G.23.d (N.W. corner of Cemetery, Arras).

   3.   Horse troughs.

     (*a*) L.12.d (close to River Scarpe. 180 Ft.).

     (*b*) L.18.d (as in 1) 300 Ft.

     (*c*) G.22.a (alongside the Bassin, Arras).

     (*d*) G.29.a.5.3 (Arras, Faub. St. Sauveur).

Water can be drawn by buckets from the River Scarpe.

B. Dumps.

Filled petrol tins (2-gallon) have been placed in all brigade and divisional dumps of divisions in the line ; 330 extra in each division dump for 37th Division.

C.   There are in addition many stand-pipes on the town supply in Arras.

The town supply will be piped forward along the Cambrai road as rapidly as possible.

D.   Extra water-carts have been allotted to the division and will be distributed to all battalions (less 8/Somersets, 11/Warwick and 13/K.R.R.C.). These will be horsed and driven under arrangements to be made by units. Harness will be provided. Particulars as to place and date when they are to be drawn will be notified later.

Nothing is to be carried on water-carts in addition to the vehicle's equipment except empty petrol tins and the oats for the animals.

E.   C.R.E. will be prepared to supplement the horse-watering arrangements given in para. 3 above, to establish a watering place for 50 animals at a time near Blangy, water being drawn from River Scarpe, and an advanced water refilling point with power pump on the Scarpe in a position dependent on progress of operations.

F.   D.A.D.O.S. will hold 30 buckets and — fathoms rope for use in wells in captured territory. A small reserve of water bottles (1,500) is also held.

G.   Owing to dangers of poison or pollution, all water (any drinkables) found in captured territory must be regarded with the greatest suspicion, and all ranks strictly cautioned against drinking it before it has been tested and passed fit for consumption, by competent M.O.'s.

H.   With reference to D.R.O. 2405 of 30th March 1917, soda tablets for sterilizing water will be issued to units at the refilling points on " Y " day. Distribution as follows :—

Divisional H.Q.	250
" B " Echelon D.A.C.	500
Each field company (500)	1,500
Each infantry brigade (5,000)	15,000
9/North Staffordshire	1,000
Divisional Train	1,000
Each field ambulance (500)	1,500
28th Mobile Veterinary Section	250
Divisional reserve	9,000
	30,000

IV.   Ordnance Stores.

(a) Demands for Ordnance Stores must be kept as low as possible, so as not to block up railheads and unnecessarily increase the transport on the roads.

(b) Stores collected at salvage dumps may be drawn by units as required, demands being made and receipts given by responsible officers.

(c) Special attention is directed to the necessity for

collecting and returning to railhead broken or unservice-
able spare gun parts.

V. Veterinary.

An advance collecting station will be furnished from
the mobile veterinary section and be situated in the vicinity
of the wheeled echelon of the first line transport, to receive
sick or wounded animals.

All sick and wounded animals will be taken over on
arrival and the men in whose charge they arrive will be
returned to their units.

VI. Remounts.

Remounts will be taken over as usual at supply railhead. If the distance between railhead and destination
exceeds one day's march, conducting parties will be provided with the necessary rations and forage at some intermediate stage.

Conducting parties will bring with them the requisite
number of head collars, the stake head collars which are
sent up with remounts from the base will be handed over
to a representative from the mobile veterinary section at
railhead.

VII. Postal.

(a) Units will draw mails at the same time and place as
supplies.

(b) Brigade field post offices will be attached to the
supply section of the train companies affiliated to them.
The N.C.O. in charge and one man will accompany the
train wagons to refilling points to distribute incoming
mails to representatives of units, and to take over outgoing
mails from the latter.

(c) When supplies are drawn by horsed transport direct
from railhead, the postal representative will attend there
with the train wagons, and accompany them to refilling
points.

(d) Whenever practicable the regular post orderlies of
each unit should attend at the refilling point to take
deliveries of mails ; otherwise the unit's representative
drawing supplies will receive and sign for the mails of
his unit. In the latter event, the representative of the
unit must be in possession of A.B. 426 (Postal Orderlies'
Receipt Book) in order that a proper system of receipt for
registered letters may be maintained.

VIII. Salvage.

(a) Major H. Y. Richardson is VI. Corps Salvage Officer—
address :

c/o Town Major,
Avesnes-le-Comte.

(b) The divisional salvage company will come under
corps control on a date to be notified later. Brigade
sections will receive orders when and where to join direct
from divisional salvage officer. All must be fully rationed
for consumption on day after joining corps salvage unit.

(*c*) Great assistance can be given to salvage work if every one will pick up and bring some article to the nearest battlefield salvage dump.

IX.   Railways and Roads.

(1) When an advance takes place, the repair of railways and roads must be put in hand at once, and units must help in any way they can.

Under no circumstances whatever are any railway permanent ways, material or buildings to be interfered with by troops. Signal sections are particularly warned against putting up lines which cross the permanent ways without ample clearance.

(2) A corps roads officer has been appointed (Captain Thomas, Avesnes-le-Comte) who supervises and directs work on roads in VI. Corps area, except the Routes Nationales—which are kept up by the French.

X.   Transport.

(*a*) If the situation permits first line transport of infantry brigades (with 12 G.S. wagons attached to each from "B" Echelon, D.A.C.), R.E., and field ambulances forming advanced dressing stations, will follow their brigades to Arras and will be parked in brigade areas as far forward as shell-fire permits.

The following sites have been selected provisionally :—

      (I) 112th Infantry Brigade G.23.d (N. of Cemetery).

    (II) 111th   ,,   ,,   G.23.c (E. of the railway siding track).

   (III) 63rd   ,,   ,,   G.23.a (S. of Blangy road).

(*b*) If transport cannot pass through Arras orders will be given at the time brigades move forward from the line of control posts west of Arras for it to park. Sites of parks have been selected as follows :—

      (I) 63rd   Infantry Brigade L.18.a ⎰between R.
    (II) 111th   ,,   ,,   L.12.b ⎱Scarpe and Arras — St. Pol main road.

   (III) 112th   ,,   ,,   G.19.b S. of rifle range.

(*c*) As soon as the transport has been parked pack trains will be organized immediately in every unit on following scale :

Field Companies R.E. 41 (including 8 from pioneers and 8 from field ambulance).

Infantry Brigade H.Q. 2
Infantry battalions . 30
M.G. Companies . 30
Pioneer battalion . 16 (excluding the 8 animals and 8 drivers to be sent to each field company before starting).

Field ambulances	.	12 (excluding the 8 animals and 4 drivers to be sent to affiliated field companies before starting).
Attached D.A.C.	.	30 (10 animals and 5 drivers to be sent to the field company in each column).

These pack trains will be organized into suitable bodies by brigade transport officers and led by the same routes as taken by brigades to the parking grounds fixed in paragraph (*a*), where they will be directed to sites for lines by the divisional transport officer. Until further notice all such pack transport will be at the disposal of brigades, field companies, and field ambulances with the exception of 16 animals and drivers of the 9/North Staffordshire (Pioneers) which will be at the disposal of the O.C. battalion.

(*d*) The loads to be carried forward will be decided by brigade etc. commanders, but must include buckets and picketing gear.

(*e*) The pack transport will be designated :—

" Pack Echelon 1st Line Transport ".

Remainder of 1st Line will be designated :—

" Wheeled Echelon 1st Line Transport ".

(*f*) Captain H. W. Cousins, 37th Divisional Train, will act as divisional transport officer. His headquarters will be Transport of H.Q.'s, 111th Infantry Brigade.

If the transport is divided as described in (*c*) his headquarters will be at the advanced divisional ration dump, G.23.a.3.2 (Blangy road) from the time the pack echelon moves forward from the wheeled echelon park.

(*g*) Train transport and H.Q.'s of " B " Echelon D.A.C. will remain parked in lines occupied on night Y/Z day, in readiness to move forward to the area given in para. (*b*) above as soon as first line transport has moved forward.

XI. Accommodation.

(*a*) The accommodation in the forward areas is restricted, and on night of Y/Z days two-thirds of the division will be in tents or bivouac shelters. Tents are being collected, for use in the forward area, but those occupied on W/X and X/Y nights together with any others that may be available, will have to be struck and moved forward with the division. Every tent in the division's present area will be taken forward.

(*b*) It is essential that all tents should be thoroughly camouflaged. " Kutch " should be demanded from Ordnance.

No white tents will be allowed to be pitched in the forward area.

Special attention is to be paid to the collection of tent pegs, valises, and peg-bags.

XII.   Blankets, valises, greatcoats, jerkins.

Brigade dumps of these articles belonging to troops going E. of Arras will be found in the areas occupied on Y/Z night at the place where tents occupied that night have been struck and dumped.

Tarpaulins for their protection have been demanded.

Blankets will be rolled in bundles of 10 securely fastened with string, spinyarn or hay-bale wire.

Valises will be packed with greatcoats and the jerkins strapped on the outside under the securing straps.

Men must be specially warned against leaving private correspondence or valuables in their valises or greatcoat pockets as it will be impossible to ensure each man receiving his own valise and greatcoat (if reissued during active operations) in the first instance.

Each unit must leave one N.C.O. and one man per company as a guard on these dumps. All to have 3 days' rations. Sites of dumps to be communicated to divisional H.Q.

XIII.   Divisional mobile canteen.

Will be moved under orders of O.C. Divisional Train.

In the forward area it will serve the 112th Infantry Brigade. Subsequently it will be placed so as to supply walking wounded, firstly W. of Arras and later E. of Arras as close to the advanced dressing station as the situation permits. Additional Soyers stoves will be drawn from D.A.D.O.S.

XIV.   Surplus baggage.

All units must have got rid of surplus baggage by noon of 4th April, after which nothing further can be received at the divisional store at Roellecourt.

Further instructions will be issued regarding the guards to be left in charge of this baggage store.

All R.E. material for training must be sent to R.E. yard at Roellecourt by 9 A.M. on 3rd instant.

Practice and dummy grenades may be sent to the Divisional School, Frévent—live explosives separated from dummies and clearly marked. It is strictly forbidden to store any live ammunition, grenades, detonators, etc. in the divisional baggage dump.

All C.O.'s will render certificates to D.H.Q. through the usual channel that none has been so dumped or left in billets.

XV.   Sanitation.

(a) The divisional commander desires every C.O. to ensure that his present billets and area are left in a state cleaner and tidier than when it was occupied. Other troops will take over immediately the division vacates the area.

(b) Owing to the congestion of troops in the forward area it is more than usually important that the strictest attention be paid to sanitation and the sanitary police work to prevent pollution of billets, bivouacs, and trenches.

XVI.   Town Majors.

The town majors, appointed in the division, with clerks, will remain in their villages.

Other personnel will, however, rejoin their units on the 4th April.

Sanitary parties to clean up villages will be left by O.'sC. units for a few hours after they have been evacuated.

R. M. AIREY,
Captain,
D.A.Q.M.G.,
37th Division.

BATTLES OF ARRAS

INSTRUCTIONS TO THE CAVALRY CORPS, THIRD ARMY No. G.S. 21/11, 3RD APRIL 1917

With reference to Third Army Order No. 173, para. 7 (i) :—

I.   The situation should become clear during the period between the time our troops reach the Brown line and the time when they are advancing to the Green line.

II.   Should it appear likely that cavalry can be employed with advantage, orders will be issued for the advance of the Cavalry Corps.

III.   The Cavalry Corps will be ready to advance from positions just west of Arras at Zero plus 6 hours, as the order to advance may be received at any time after that hour.

IV.   It is the intention to issue this order in such time as will enable the leading brigades of the cavalry divisions to pass through the Green line as soon as, or very shortly after, the infantry reach that line, where the infantry are timed to arrive at Zero plus 12 hours.

V.   The telephone or telegraphic order will be—
" Cavalry advance ".

VI.   The Cavalry Corps will maintain close touch with the VI Corps and must know in what way the VI Corps intend to use their Corps Mounted Troops.

VII.   The first objective of the Cavalry Corps will be the front, Chérisy, Vis-en-Artois, Boiry-Notre-Dame.

As soon as the Cavalry Corps is relieved by the infantry of the VI and VII Corps or by the infantry of the 17th Division (attached to the Cavalry Corps) on this front, the Cavalry Corps will advance to the front Cagnicourt, Dury, Étaing.

Should the enemy be in retreat, touch will be maintained by patrols.

VIII.   Should the operations result in the Green line being reached by the infantry at Zero plus 12 hours, it is intended that the first objective of the cavalry should be reached before dark.

L. J. BOLS,
Major-General,
General Staff, Third Army.

BATTLES OF ARRAS

INSTRUCTIONS TO 1st BRIGADE, HEAVY BRANCH, MACHINE GUN CORPS, THIRD ARMY No. G.S. 8/31, 3rd APRIL 1917

Reference Third Army Order No. 173 of the 1st inst.

1.   1st Brigade, Heavy Branch, Machine Gun Corps, will co-operate in the attack of the Third Army on the Blue and Brown lines.

2.   Tanks and their personnel are distributed to Corps as follows :—

    VI. Corps—Blue line—16 Tanks C Battn.
                Brown line and Green line—20 Tanks C Battn.
    VII. Corps—Blue line— 4 Tanks C Battn.
                   12   „   D   „
                Brown and Green lines—12 Tanks D Battn.
  XVII. Corps—Blue, Brown and Green lines—8 Tanks C Battn.
    After the Blue line has been gained, 4 tanks will be transferred from the VII. Corps to VI. Corps to operate against the Brown line.

3.   Tanks are operating on a plan co-ordinated for the whole Army front against selected objectives such as the valley south-west of the Bois de la Maison Blanche, the Railway Triangle east of Blangy, the line of Redoubts between the Railway Triangle and Tilloy-lez-Mofflaines, Tilloy-lez-Mofflaines and the Harp.   After the Blue line has been captured, rallying points have been chosen and from these all available Tanks will move forward with the infantry to the capture of the Brown and Green lines.

    In carrying out these plans, Tank detachments will be placed under the orders of Corps Commanders in whose areas they are working, and all details have already been arranged direct between Corps Commanders and the 1st Brigade, Heavy Branch, M.G.C.

    The general lines of advance, objectives and rallying points are shown on the attached map.[1]

    If for any reason, such as unfavourable weather or impassable ground, Tank detachments are unable to carry out their allotted

[1] Not printed.

tasks, they will come into Corps reserve and must not be used again without reference to Army Headquarters.

4.   O.C. 1st Brigade, Heavy Branch, M.G. Corps, will act as adviser to Corps Commanders, will communicate with them on all matters of detail, and will send them his operation orders. His headquarters will be at Montenescourt.

CHARLES GRANT, Lt.-Colonel,
General Staff, Third Army.

BATTLES OF ARRAS

VI. CORPS OPERATION ORDER No. 100, 3RD APRIL 1917

Enemy's forces.

1.   To the south of Arras the enemy has fallen back with his
main forces to the Hindenburg Line.
        Four German divisions hold the front from Croisilles to
Roclincourt.   Of these, about 4 battalions hold the front from
Tilloy-lez-Mofflaines to the River Scarpe, with 7 or 8 companies
drawn from 3 battalions in front line.

Our forces.

2.   The Fifth Army and the VII. Corps on the right of the Third
Army have advanced and are now facing the enemy on the
Hindenburg Line.
        The Third Army and the First Army are to break through
the enemy's defences on the front Croisilles—Givenchy.   The
Third Army is then to capture the enemy's defensive system which
runs from Arras to Cambrai (Hindenburg Line).   The Fifth Army
is to co-operate with the Third Army at a date subsequent to Z
day.
        The bombardment of the enemy's positions is to take place
on V, W, X, Y days and the assault will be made on Z day.
        All corps will advance simultaneously to the assault of the
various objectives.
        The VII. Corps attacks on the right and the XVII. Corps on
the left of the VI. Corps.
        The date of Z day and Zero hour will be issued later.

Rôle of VI. Corps.

3.   The VI. Corps will break through the enemy's defences as
shown on objective map already issued.   The 3rd, 12th and 15th
Divisions are responsible for the capture of the Black, Blue and
Brown lines.   The 37th Division is responsible for the capture
of the Green line.

Rôle of divisions.

4.   The 3rd, 12th and 15th Divisions will assault the enemy's
front line system simultaneously at Zero hour.
        The advance from the Black line will commence at Zero

plus 2 hours, and from the Blue line at Zero plus 6 hours 40 minutes.

After the Brown line is captured the 37th Division will pass through the leading divisions and will advance at Zero plus 10 hours to the Green line, which will be reached at Zero plus 12 hours.

Each objective will be firmly consolidated immediately it is captured. Units will be reorganized as rapidly as possible so that troops may be available for further action or to resist counter-attacks.

Gas drums.

5.   Gas drums will be fired on to the enemy's second system at 6.15 A.M. on V day.

Preliminary bombardment.

6.   The bombardment on V, W and X days will commence as follows :

> V day 6.30 A.M.
> W day 6 A.M.
> X day 5 A.M.

On Y day the hour the bombardment will begin will be notified later.

7.   The schemes for the co-operation of the 1st Brigade, Heavy Branch, M.G.C. and Special Companies R.E. have already been issued.

8.   Corps headquarters will remain at Noyelle-Vion.

9.   Acknowledge.

LOCH,

Issued at 1.50 P.M.   B.G.G.S.

BATTLES OF ARRAS

G.H.Q. LETTER O.A.D. 381,
4TH APRIL 1917

To

First Army.
Third Army.
Fifth Army.
Cavalry Corps.

1.   After the Cavalry Corps, consisting of the 1st, 2nd and 3rd Cavalry Divisions, have concentrated in the Third Army area, in accordance with O.A. 618, dated April 1st, the command of these three divisions and the 4th Cavalry Division will be exercised as follows :—

 (i)   The Cavalry Corps Headquarters and the 2nd and 3rd Cavalry Divisions will be under the direct orders of the G.O.C. Third Army.

 (ii)   The 1st Cavalry Division will be administered by the Cavalry Corps Headquarters but will be held in G.H.Q. Reserve.

 (iii)   The 4th Cavalry Division will be under the direct orders of the G.O.C. Fifth Army.

2.   The rôle of the Cavalry in the forthcoming operations on the fronts of the First, Third and Fifth Armies will be as follows :—

 (a)   The Cavalry Corps, consisting of Corps H.Q., and the 2nd and 3rd Cavalry Divisions (to which the Third Army is attaching the 17th Division), will be held in readiness to be employed by the G.O.C. Third Army according to circumstances, with a view to exploiting a break through the enemy's lines east of Arras.

 (b)   The 4th Cavalry Division will be employed by the G.O.C. Fifth Army to exploit any break in the enemy's lines east of Croisilles.

      In the event of the 2nd, 3rd and 4th Cavalry Divisions breaking the enemy's line as stated above, the 4th Cavalry Division would come under the orders of the Cavalry Corps at a later stage of the battle under instructions which would be issued by G.H.Q.

(c)   The 1st Cavalry Division will be used under the orders of G.H.Q. either to reinforce the Cavalry Corps east of Arras or to reinforce the First Army in order to exploit a success north of the Scarpe.

3.   Should the development of the operations render it preferable to advance the mass of the Cavalry through the Fifth rather than the Third Army front, the 4th Cavalry Division may be reinforced directly by either the 2nd or 3rd Cavalry Division, or by both, according to circumstances.   Such reinforcement, together with the Cavalry Corps Headquarters, would then be placed temporarily under the orders of the G.O.C. Fifth Army by instructions from G.H.Q.

L. E. KIGGELL,
Lieut.-General,
G.H.Q.   Chief of the General Staff.

BATTLES OF ARRAS

1ST BRIGADE HEAVY BRANCH MACHINE GUN CORPS OPERATION ORDER No. 3, 4TH APRIL 1917

1. Reference Third Army Order No. 173 and attached map.[1] Tanks will be employed in conjunction with the Third Army as follows :—

2. Allotment. Tanks will be allotted as follows :—
   XVII. Corps.   8 tanks, " C " Battalion.
   VI. Corps.   16 tanks, " C " Battalion.
   VII. Corps.   16 tanks, " C " Battalion (4 tanks).
                              " D " Battalion (12 tanks).

3. Headquarters.
   1st Brigade Heavy Branch, Montenescourt.
   " C " Battalion, Arras (Convent de Notre Dame, Rue Baudimont).
   " D " Battalion, Arras (Convent de Notre Dame).

4. Starting Points.
   XVII. Corps.   Roclincourt for tanks operating against Bois de la Maison Blanche. Forrestier Redoubt (G.17a central) for tanks operating against the villages of Laurent-Blangy and Athies.
   VI. Corps.   Arras Cemetery (southern edge) for tanks operating against Railway Triangle and redoubts north of Tilloy-lez-Mofflaines.
                  St. Sauveur for tanks operating against the village of Tilloy-lez-Mofflaines.
                  Point M.5c.15.85 for tanks operating against the Harp.
   VII. Corps.   Beaurains for tanks operating against Telegraph Hill and Neuville-Vitasse.
                  Mercatel for tanks operating against trench junction in Square N.27a & b.[2]

---

[1] Not reproduced. Sketch 5 shows the plan of the main tank attack, together with starting and rallying points. Positions of rallying points not shown on the sketch are given in footnotes below.
[2] Junction of Hindenburg and Wancourt-Feuchy Lines.

5. <u>Starting Times.</u> All tanks except the four at Mercatel will leave their starting points at Zero hour, and will align themselves with the infantry on the Black line at Zero plus 2 hours.

The four tanks at Mercatel will leave their starting point in time to align themselves with the infantry on the Blue line at Zero plus 6 hours 40 minutes.

6. Objectives, Blue line.

XVII. Corps. (a) 4 tanks on the valley west and south-west of Bois de la Maison Blanche.

      (b) 2 tanks on the village of Laurent-Blangy and the railway embankment east of Hervin Farm, thence northwards up the valley.

      (c) 2 tanks move towards Athies (Brown line).

VI. Corps. (d) 2 tanks on the Railway Triangle.

      (e) 2 tanks on the line of redoubts north of Tilloy-lez-Mofflaines (i.e. Hamel Work, Heron Work, Holt Work, Hotte Work, and Houlette Work).

      (f) 4 tanks on the village of Tilloy-lez-Mofflaines (2 round north and 2 round south of village).

      (g) 8 tanks on the Harp and Noisy Work.[1]

VII. Corps. (h) 4 tanks on the Harp.

      (i) 4 tanks on Telegraph Hill and the Hindenburg Line between Telegraph Hill and Neuville-Vitasse.

      (j) 4 tanks on Neuville-Vitasse (2 round north and 2 round south of the village).

      (k) 4 tanks remain in Mercatel.

7. <u>Rallying Points</u> (for tanks operating against Blue line).

XVII. Corps. No. 1 Point, H.7b.4.3 [2] for tanks (a) and (b)—tanks under (c) nil.

VI. Corps. No. 2 Point, H.19d.9.8 for tanks (d).

      No. 3 Point, H.31d.5.6 for tanks (e) and (f).

      No. 4 Point, N.1d.7.8 for tanks (g).

VII. Corps. No. 4 Point, N.1d.7.8 for tanks (h) which from this point come under VI. Corps.

      No. 5 Point, N.20a.1.6 [3] for tanks (i) and (j)—tanks under (k) nil.

8. <u>Objectives, Brown line.</u> The advance from the Blue line will take place at Zero plus 6 hours 40 minutes.

XVII. Corps. (l) Tanks rallied at Point No. 1 on the Point du Jour, thence southwards down Keen, Kick, and Opium Trenches to Athies.

      (m) 2 tanks on village of Athies.

VI. Corps. (n) Tanks rallied at Point No. 2 will move on with the infantry to Feuchy Redoubt, thence down the Wancourt-Feuchy Line to Feuchy Chapel.

---

[1] The work on the eastern side of the Harp.

[2] Just east of the railway, 700 yards south of Bois de la Maison Blanche.   [3] The eastern outskirts of Neuville-Vitasse.

(*o*) Tanks rallied at Point No. 3 and Point No. 4 will move on with the infantry to Feuchy Chapel Redoubt, and after the capture of this work will divide into two parts and proceed north and south along the Wancourt —Feuchy Line.

VII. Corps. (*p*) Tanks rallied at Point No. 5 will move on with the infantry to the Brown line at Wancourt Cemetery.

(*q*) Tanks from Mercatel (*k*) will move on with the infantry to trench junction N.27.a & b.

9. Rallying Points (for tanks operating against Brown line).

XVII. Corps. No. 6 Point, H.14b.7.7 [1] for tanks (*l*) & (*m*).
VI. Corps. No. 7 Point, N.3b.9.9 for tanks (*n*) and (*o*).
VII. Corps. No. 8 Point, N.22a.8.6 [2] for tanks (*p*) & (*q*).

10. Objectives, Green line. The advance from the Brown line will take place at Zero plus 10 hours.

Tanks rallied at Points 7 & 8 will move on with the 37th Division against Monchy-le-Preux, the tanks from No. 8 rallying point proceeding via Wancourt and Guémappe.

This forward movement is dependent on the possibility of getting forward supplies of petrol and water to rallying points No. 7 & 8.

11. Dumps. Dumps will be established at G.15b.5.8,[3] Achicourt, Beaurains.

12. Refilling Points. Refilling points will be established as soon as possible after the Brown line has fallen at N.3b.9.9 and N.22a.8.6.[4]

13. Routes. Detail of exact routes to be followed are being arranged with divisions concerned by tank battalions direct.

14. Synchronization of Watches. An officer from Brigade Headquarters will visit headquarters of battalions and detached companies daily between the hours of 2 and 4 P.M. for the purpose of giving correct time.

15. Z day and Zero hour will be notified later.

16. Acknowledge.

C. D. BAKER CARR,
Colonel,
Commanding 1st Brigade H.B.M.G.C.

Issued at 3 P.M.

---

[1] The northern outskirts of Athies.
[2] On the Wancourt-Feuchy Line due west of Wancourt.
[3] North-west of St. Nicholas, the Arras suburb north of the Scarpe.
[4] At Rallying Points No. 7 and 8 respectively.

BATTLES OF ARRAS

3RD DIVISION OPERATION ORDER No. 147, 4TH APRIL 1917

1. Enemy's Forces.

    To the south of Arras the enemy has fallen back with his main forces to the Hindenburg Line.

    Four German Divisions hold the front from Croisilles to Roclincourt. Of these about 4 battalions hold the front from Tilloy-lez-Mofflaines to the River Scarpe, with 7 or 8 companies drawn from 3 battalions in front line.

2. Our Forces.

    (*a*) The Fifth Army and VII. Corps on the right of the Third Army have advanced and are now facing the enemy on the Hindenburg Line.

    (*b*) The First and Third Armies are about to assume the offensive with the object of breaking through the enemy's defences and capturing the enemy's defensive system which runs from Arras to Cambrai (Hindenburg Line).

3. VI. Corps Objective.

    The VI. Corps will break through the enemy's defences between the northern half of the Harp (inclusive) to the River Scarpe.

    The VII. Corps attacks on the right and the XVII. Corps on the left of the VI. Corps.

4.   The VI. Corps will attack on " Z " Day with three Divisions in the line and one in reserve.

5. Order of Battle.

    (*a*) The 3rd Division will attack on the right, the 12th Division in the centre, and the 15th Division on the left of the VI. Corps.

    (*b*) The 14th Division (VII. Corps) will be attacking on the right of the 3rd Division.

6. Frontage of Attack.

    (*a*) The front of the VI. Corps will be from the road in G.35.b to the River Scarpe.

    (*b*) The 3rd Division is allotted a frontage of attack from G.35.b.8.0 to G.30.c.8.2.

7. 3rd Divn. Boundaries.

The boundaries of the 3rd Division in the attack will be as follows :—

Southern Boundary (between 3rd Divn. & 14th Divn. [VII. Corps]).

G.35.b.8.0—G.36.c.2.7—M.6.b.$\frac{1}{2}$.9—thence along the road to N.7.b.5.8—N.8.d.9.5—thence a straight line to the German third system at N.16.b.0.3.

Northern Boundary (between 3rd and 12th Divisions).

G.30.c.8.2 — G.30.d.2$\frac{1}{2}$.$\frac{1}{2}$ — H.31.a.1.6$\frac{1}{2}$ — H.31.a.4.4 — thence along the road to H.31.d.5.9$\frac{1}{2}$—N.3.d.4$\frac{1}{2}$.7—thence a straight line to the German third system.[1]

8. 3rd Divn. Objectives.

The 3rd Division is allotted Objectives as follows :—

1st Objective (Black line)—The German front system of trenches : trench line G.36.c.9.1 — G.36.c.9.4 — G.36.b.5.0 — G.36.d.8.9—Eastern edge of Devil's Wood.

2nd Objective (Blue line)—The German second system of trenches : Noisy Redoubt—trench line N.1.d.3.0—N.1.d.2.3—N.1.d.4.9 — N.1.a.9$\frac{1}{2}$.4 — N.1.b.1.6 — H.31.d.6.4 — H.31.d.9.4 — H.32.c.1.7.

3rd Objective (Brown line)—German third system, Wancourt—Feuchy Line, included in the Divisional Boundaries.

9. G.O.C.'s Intention.

It is the G.O.C.'s intention to secure all the three Objectives.

10. Allotment of Objectives.

(a) To the 76th Inf. Bde. (less 1 Bn.) is entrusted the task of capturing and consolidating the 1st Objective.

(b) To the 9th Inf. Bde. is entrusted the task of capturing and consolidating the 2nd Objective.

A battalion of the 76th Inf. Bde. will be attached to the 9th Inf. Bde. to assist it in carrying out its task and will join the 9th Inf. Bde. on Y/Z night under orders to be issued by G.O.C. 9th Inf. Bde.

(c) The 8th Inf. Bde. is entrusted with the task of capturing and consolidating the 3rd Objective.

11. (i) During consolidation G.O.sC. Inf. Bdes. will pay special attention to the construction of strong points.

(ii) The 9th Inf. Bde. will detail a commandant and suitable garrison for Tilloy Village and will have it put in a state of defence as soon as possible after the capture of the 2nd Objective.

(iii) C.R.E. will detail parties for ramping the enemy's trenches where necessary for the passage of guns.

12. Communication Trenches.

(a) Between 6 P.M. on night Y/Z and Zero hour on " Z " Day the Crinchon Sewer, Godley's Avenue and all C.T.'s will be reserved for use of Infantry Bdes. moving forward to their

---

[1] These co-ordinates can be disregarded, as the boundaries are shown on Map 5. Similarly, as regards the objectives which follow, the Black, Blue, and Brown lines are shown. (Compiler's note.)

positions of assembly. No other traffic will be permitted between these hours, except the move of two companies 8th Inf. Bde. from the front line after relief.

8th, 9th and 76th Inf. Bdes. will post the necessary sentries in their areas to enforce this order.

(b) After Zero hour on " Z " Day Imperial and Iceland Streets will be used as " In " C.T.'s, Twenty and Fifteen Streets will be used as " Out " Communication Trenches.

13. **Preliminary Bombardment.**

The preliminary bombardment will last for 4 days, commencing on " V " Day.

The bombardment on 5th and 6th April will commence as follows :—

> 5th April—6.0 A.M.
> 6th April—5.0 A.M.

14. **Arty. & Infy. Bridges and Ramps.**

On the night Y/Z the following will be carried out :—

(a) G.O.'sC. 9th and 76th Inf. Bdes. will arrange to place the necessary ladders and infantry bridges in position in their own areas.

(b) C.R.E. will arrange to place any necessary artillery bridges in position and will arrange for the removal of barricades on the Cambrai Road east of the Rue du Temple, for the passage of Tanks.

(c) The shafts in the tunnel immediately south of the Cambrai Road will be opened up by the New Zealand Tunnelling Company under arrangements to be made between 76th Inf. Bde. and N.Z. Tunnelling Company.

The G.O.C. 76th Inf. Bde. will detail Lewis Gun detachments to sweep the enemy's front line parapet from these shafts immediately the artillery barrage opens.

15. **Relief of Battalion in the Line.**

(a) On the night Y/Z the 76th Inf. Bde. will take over the line from the 8th Inf. Bde. Relief to be completed by 8.0 P.M.

(b) The battalion of the 8th Inf. Bde. in the line will after relief rejoin its brigade, under orders of the G.O.C. 8th Inf. Bde.

16. **Forward Move to Positions of Assembly.**

(a) On the night Y/Z the 9th and 76th Inf. Bdes. and 8th Inf. Bde. (less 2 Bns.) will move forward in accordance with either attached Tables " A ", " B," or " C ", as may be ordered, so that by Zero minus 1 hour on " Z " Day they will be formed up in their assembly trenches.[1]

If the forward move is ordered both overland and underground, the 76th Inf. Bde. will move overland and the 9th Inf. Bde. underground, in accordance with attached Table " C ".

(b) When Brigades are ready assembled in their positions of assembly they will report the fact to Divisional H.Q. by telephone and wire. The code word to be used will be the name of the Brigadier.

---

[1] Not printed. " A " was overground, " B " underground, and " C " partly overground and partly underground. " B " was that adopted. (Compiler's note.)

17. **Disposition of Troops at Zero.**

At Zero hour on " Z " Day Brigades will then be disposed as follows :—

76th Inf. Bde. (less 1 Bn.) } In assembly trenches between the Front and Reserve Line (exclusive).

9th Inf. Bde. 1 Bn. 76th Inf. Bde. } In assembly trenches between the Reserve Line (inclusive) and the Rue du Temple.

8th Inf. Bde. { 2 Battalions in assembly trenches west of the Rue du Temple. 2 Battalions in Ronville Caves. M.G. Coy. in position for opening M.G. barrage.

18. **R.E. Coys. allotted to Inf. Bdes.**

On " Z " Day the following R.E. will be placed at the disposal of Inf. Bdes. for consolidation and will move forward under orders to be issued by G.O.sC. Brigades concerned.

56th Field Coy. R.E. to 9th Inf. Bde.

2 Secs. Ches. Field Coy. R.E. to 8th Inf. Bde.

2 Secs. East Riding Field Coy. R.E. to 76th Inf. Bde.

The remainder of the Field Companies and the Pioneer Battalion will be at the disposal of the C.R.E.

19. **The Assault.**

(a) At Zero hour on " Z " Day the 76th Inf. Bde. will assault with three battalions.

(b) Simultaneously with the advance of the leading infantry the artillery and machine-gun barrages will be formed.

(c) The 8th Inf. Bde. will be in Divisional Reserve and in the event of the 76th Inf. Bde. requiring assistance the G.O.C. Division will reinforce from the 8th Inf. Bde., keeping the 9th Inf. Bde. intact for its attack on the Second Objective.

(d) The G.O.C. 9th Inf. Bde. will time his advance so that his Brigade passes through the 76th Inf. Bde. on the First Objective at Zero plus 2 hours without making any appreciable halt on the First Objective.

(e) When the 9th Inf. Bde. has passed through, the G.O.C. 76th Inf. Bde. will consolidate the First Objective with his Brigade (less 1 Bn.) and will form the Divisional Reserve.

After the capture of the first objective the G.O.C. 76th Inf. Bde. will at once re-form his Brigade and hold it in readiness to assist the 9th Inf. Bde. in case of necessity.

Should it be necessary to employ the 76th Inf. Bde. to reinforce the 9th Inf. Bde., the 8th Inf. Bde. will be prepared to occupy the position captured by 76th Inf. Bde. with one battalion.

(f) The G.O.C. 8th Inf. Bde. will time his advance so that his Brigade passes through the 9th Inf. Bde. on the Second Objective at Zero plus 6 hours and 40 minutes without making any appreciable halt on the Second Objective.

(g) As soon as the Third Objective has been captured the Division in Corps Reserve will pass through the leading Divisions of the Corps with the object of securing the line Guémappe— Monchy-le-Preux.

K

20.   During the attack each Inf. Bde. will have the direct call on one battery through the Liaison Artillery Officer attached to Brigade H.Q.

The Divisional Commander can call direct on the Heavy Artillery Group affiliated to the Division in case of necessity.

21. Artillery Barrage.

During the attack troops must follow close up under the artillery barrage.

22. Re-bombardment.

In the event of a considerable section of the advance being held up and re-bombardment being necessary, application must be made to Divisional H.Q. who will arrange with the Corps Artillery, and fix the hour at which the re-bombardment will commence. The bombardment will last 30 minutes from the hour named, and it must be clearly understood that the infantry must assault at " Zero plus 30 minutes ". The last two minutes of the re-bombardment will be very intense, in order to warn the infantry.

23. Tanks.

Tanks will be used for the attack on the Second Objective.

These will be concentrated behind our front line system and will move forward so as to cross the First Objective with the 9th Inf. Bde. as it moves forward to the assault.

24. Hostile Batteries.

As soon as the Second Objective is gained a large number of the enemy's gun positions will be within effective rifle range.

Arrangements will be made with the 9th Inf. Bde. to keep them under constant rifle and machine-gun fire.

25. Forward Move of Batteries.

The advance of certain batteries to support the attack of the 8th Inf. Bde. on the Third Objective will be carried out in accordance with instructions issued separately to the C.R.A.

26. Contact Aeroplanes.

Aeroplanes working with the VI. Corps will be marked with one black band under both lower planes ; streamers will be attached to each plane immediately behind the black bands.

These machines will be constantly in the air during " Z " Day and the infantry must be warned to look out for signals.

27. Flares & Flags.

(a) Flares to indicate to aeroplanes the positions reached by our leading infantry will be lit as the different objectives are reached, and whenever called for by contact aeroplanes by means of the Klaxon Horn or the firing of a white light.

(b) Two N.C.O.'s or selected men per platoon will carry yellow and black flags. These will be waved to indicate to our artillery observers the position of the leading infantry.

These flags are on no account to be planted in the ground, and must not be waved by troops who know that they are not our most advanced line.

28. **S.O.S. Signal.**

    The S.O.S. Signal during the operations will be :—

    A Succession of Green Lights.

29. **Communications.**

    (*a*) Each Inf. Bde. will arrange to carry forward at least one telephone cable with each assaulting battalion. These lines will be connected with the buried cables at the ends of the tunnels.

    (*b*) In addition each Bde. will arrange to establish visual signalling stations on arrival at their Objectives, to communicate with stations which will be established near our front line in G.36.d and in the Harp in N.1.d.

    (*c*) Each Brigade, Battalion, and Company will organize a service of runners.

    (*d*) 3rd Divisional Signals will arrange a supply of pigeons to be carried forward with Battalion H.Q. of assaulting Battalions.

    (*e*) 3rd Divisional Signals will arrange for the organization of wireless communication in accordance with the instructions contained in Instructions No. 2. (Addendum to S. 733.)

30. **Medical.**

    Advanced Dressing Stations are established at the Girls' School, Rue du Temple and in the Caves at the junction of the Rue du Temple & Rue St. Quentin.

31. **Divisional and R.E. Dumps.**

    (*a*) The Advanced Divisional Dump is established in Aladdin's Cave in the Rue de Rietz (G.29.c.6.9).

    (*b*) Advanced R.E. Dumps are established as follows :—

No. 1 R.E. Dump—In shell craters between old British front and support lines and 15th & 16th St.

No. 2 R.E. Dump—West of and close to Strafe Wood and south of and close to Imperial Street.

32. **Synchronization of Watches.**

    Watches will be synchronized with the General Staff, 3rd Division, at 3.0 P.M. on " Y " Day and at 1.0 A.M. on " Z " Day.

33. **Brigade H.Q.**

    Brigade H.Q. are established as follows :—

        8th Inf. Bde.—Dugouts in King Street (G.29.d.4.6).

        9th Inf. Bde.—Dugouts in King Street (G.30.c.1.1).

        76th Inf. Bde.—Dugouts in Tunnel (G.35.b.8½.6).

34. **Divisional H.Q.**

    Advanced Divisional H.Q. and H.Q. Divisional Arty., and C.R.E. will be established in Russell Cave (G.28.d.1.2) at 12 noon on " Y " Day.

35. **" Z " Day Zero Hour.**

    " Z " Day and Zero hour will be communicated separately.

36. **Acknowledge.**

W. H. TRAILL,
Lieut.-Colonel,
General Staff, 3rd Division.

BATTLES OF ARRAS

FIRST ARMY ORDER No. 103, 5TH APRIL 1917

On the assumption that the attack on the Vimy Ridge reaches its objective on Z day, the Army Commander has decided to attack and capture the Pimple and Bois en Hache with the Canadian and I. Corps respectively ; the attack to be carried out on the night of Z/Z + 1 days ; at an hour to be decided by the G.O.C. Canadian Corps in consultation with the G.O.C. I. Corps.

2.   G.O.C. Canadian Corps, will assume command of the line as far north as the Souchez River (exclusive) at 6 A.M. on Z day, and the battalion of the 24th Division, I. Corps, holding the line south of the Souchez River, will come under the orders of the G.O.C. Canadian Corps, at that hour.   This battalion will be relieved in the front line by the Canadian Corps on the evening of Z day and will be in support to the attack on the Pimple.

3.   The XIII. Corps will place two battalions of 188th Infantry Brigade, 63rd Division, at the disposal of G.O.C. I. Corps.   These two battalions will be employed as follows :—

   (*a*)   1 battalion to relieve a battalion of 73rd Infantry Brigade, 24th Division, for purposes of defence, on the night of Z – 2/ Z – 1 days.

   (*b*)   1 battalion to form a reserve to the attack on the Bois en Hache.

4.   Definite orders as to whether the attack is to take place or not will be issued from Army Headquarters on Z day.

J. BRIND, Lieut.-Colonel,
for Major-General,
General Staff, First Army.

BATTLES OF ARRAS

12TH INFANTRY BRIGADE OPERATION ORDER No. 21, 6TH APRIL 1917

1.　　　The XVII. Corps is attacking the German position immediately north of the River Scarpe at an hour, Zero, on April 9th as part of a general attack by the Third Army.

　　　The primary object of the operations is to establish a line along the German 3rd system of trenches (shewn by the Brown line on Tracing A).[1]

　　　The VI. Corps is attacking south of the River Scarpe.

2.　　　The 9th Division is attacking immediately north of the River Scarpe and is to capture the Black, Blue, and Brown lines.

　　　When the Brown line is captured the 4th Division is to pass through the 9th Division, capture the German 4th system of trenches and the village of Fampoux, and establish itself on the Green line (vide Tracing A).[1]

3.　　　The attack by the 4th Division is to be carried out by the 12th Infantry Brigade on the right and the 11th Infantry Brigade on the left. The 10th Infantry Brigade is in divisional reserve.

4.　　　The 12th Infantry Brigade will attack with three battalions in the line as follows :—

　　　　　Right : 1/King's Own.
　　　　　Centre : 2/Lancs. Fus.
　　　　　Left : 2/Essex.

5.　　　3 machine guns of 12th M.G. Coy. will be allotted to each of the three assaulting battalions.

　　　1 Stokes mortar of the 12th T.M. Battery will be allotted to each of the 2/Lancs. Fus. and 2/Essex, and 3 Stokes mortars to the 1/King's Own.

　　　The remaining 3 mortars of the 12th T.M. Battery will remain at Y Huts.

6.　　　The brigade reserve will consist of the 2/W. Riding Regt. and the 12th M.G. Coy. (less 9 guns) under the command of the O.C. 2/W. Riding Regt.

---

[1] The tracing is not reproduced, but the Brown line is shown on Map 6.

7.   The brigade and battalion boundaries are shown on Tracing A [1] and are as under :—

.   .   .   .

8.   (a) On receipt of orders from Brigade H.Q. the brigade will move out from the assembly area to the assaulting positions on the Brown line by the following routes :—

.   .   .   .

(b) The formation in which battalions advance from the assembly area will be left to the discretion of battalion commanders.

9.   On reaching the Brown line battalions will form up approximately as follows :—

.   .   .   .

10.   (a) The timings of the barrages are given in Appendix B and shewn on attached Map B.[2]

(b) A salvo of shrapnel will be fired from all 18-pdrs. to mark the start of each stage of the infantry attack ; otherwise the ammunition employed will be 50% shrapnel and 50% H.E.

(c) The " protective " barrage will be placed 300 yards in advance of the line held.

(d) From the Brown line to the 4th German system the creeping barrage will advance at 100 yards in 2 minutes, the time of starting being calculated to allow the infantry to get within 50 yards of it.

(e) Beyond the 4th German system there will be no creeping barrage, but fire will be concentrated on selected points, lifting when the infantry advancing at 100 yards in 2 minutes is within 400-500 yards.

(f) A special howitzer barrage will move through Fampoux at the rate of 100 yards in 4 minutes, thus giving the infantry passing along the northern face time to get beyond and round it before the barrage lifts from the village.

(g) A protective gun barrage will be placed along the western edge of Fampoux. It will remain till 5 minutes after the hour fixed for the advance of the infantry to cover the latter whilst they get close up to the village.

11. The attack will be carried out in accordance with the time table in Appendix A, and will be divided into two phases :—

(a) The capture of the German 4th system of trenches running north from the River Scarpe west of Fampoux to H.10.d.70.

(b) The capture of Fampoux and the establishment of a defensive line approximately from the railway bridge H.18.d.32 [3] to Hyderabad Redoubt, along the Green line.

12.   (a) At Zero +9 hrs. 45 mins. the standing barrage 300 yards in front of the Brown line will commence to advance at the rate of 100 yards in two minutes north of the Athies—Fampoux road.

[1] The tracing is not reproduced, but the Brown line is ǀshown on Map 6.

[2] This map is not reproduced, but the appendix is.

[3] The over-bridge where the Rœux—Fampoux road crosses the railway.

South of the road it will move forward at the same time but at a slower rate until parallel to the 4th German system, and will then advance throughout its length at the rate of 100 yards in 2 minutes.

(*b*) If the wind is not unfavourable a smoke barrage will be placed on the 4th German system during this time.

(*c*) The assaulting infantry will follow the barrage as closely as possible.

(*d*) The brigade reserve will move off at the same time as the 1/King's Own, i.e., Zero + 9 hrs. 40 mins.

It will keep in touch with the 1/King's Own without actually committing itself to the attack. It will, however, be prepared at any time to support the attack without further orders from Brigade H.Q.

13.　　(*a*) As soon as the German 4th system is captured posts will be pushed forward as follows as far as the barrage allows :—

1/King's Own	.	To the western outskirts of Fampoux.
2/Lancs. Fus.	.	To the sunken road from H.17.a.90 to H.17.a.89 [1] and if possible beyond this to the north-east of Fampoux, in order to cut off the enemy's retreat from the village.
2/Essex	. .	To the same line as the 2/Lancs. Fus.

(*b*) Lewis guns will be sent forward to these points.

(*c*) Troops will not enter Fampoux at this stage.

14.　　(*a*) There will be a halt of half an hour on the German 4th system, during which the brigade reserve will close up on the 1/King's Own and will get into position ready to assault Fampoux.

(*b*) While, however, the closest touch should be kept with the 1/King's Own by the brigade reserve, touch must also be maintained with the 2/Lancs. Fus. and the 2/Essex, and the commander of the brigade reserve must be prepared on his own initiative to support either of these battalions at any stage if necessary.

15.　　As soon as the brigade reserve has passed through them, the 1/King's Own will become the brigade reserve and will be prepared to act in an exactly similar way.

16.　　The chief task of the Stokes mortars allotted to the 1/King's Own will be the bombardment of Fampoux, but they will go forward later when the 2/W. Riding Regt. have passed through and will come under the orders of the O.C. 2/W. Riding Regt.

17.　　(*a*) At Zero + 10 hrs. 46 mins. a special howitzer barrage will commence to move through Fampoux at the rate of 100 yards in 4 minutes, reaching the eastern edge 32 minutes later.

(*b*) The 2/W. Riding Regt. will advance at Zero + 10 hrs. 42 mins. and will follow this barrage up through the village.

The 2/Lancs. Fus. and 2/Essex will at the same time advance to the Green line, leaving behind in the 4th German system their original 1st wave to carry on consolidation.

[1] The road running north from the centre of Fampoux towards Bailleul, for a distance of 500 yards north of the village.

(c) The 2/W. Riding Regt. will detail a company to pass rapidly along the northern edge of Fampoux and to enter it from the north and east as soon as the barrage lifts.

18.   As soon as the Green line is reached strong patrols will be pushed out to capture any artillery in the vicinity and to maintain touch with the enemy.

Touch will also be maintained with the VI. Corps south of the River Scarpe and the 11th Infantry Brigade on the left.

19.   Battalions must be prepared at any time, in the event of the attack being held up on either of their flanks, to form and consolidate defensive flanks and to push on and endeavour to turn the obstacle.

20.   The 1/King's Own and 2/W. Riding Regt. will be prepared to assist the VI. Corps by sweeping the slopes south of the River Scarpe with machine-gun fire should favourable targets present themselves.

21.   (a) The organization of a defensive line approximately along the Green line will be taken in hand at once. The line itself will be on the western slopes of the ridge, but posts will be pushed forward to obtain observation east of the ridge.

(b) Strong points will be constructed in rear of the Green line approximately as follows :—

2/W. Riding Regt. . . .	H.18.d.22.
1/King's Own . . .	H.18.c.88.
2/Lancs. Fus. . . .	H.18.a.55.
2/Essex	H.12.c.51.[1]

22.   A N.C.O. from the 9th Field Company R.E. will report to each battalion at 6 P.M. on April 8th and will be attached to Battalion H.Q. When the Green line is reached they will be sent forward to help lay out the strong points. When they have completed the laying out of the strong points they will be sent back to Brigade H.Q. when battalion commanders consider it suitable, and as soon as practicable will guide a half section 9th Field Company R.E. with a party carrying wire to each of the strong points at H.18.c.88 and at H.12.c.51.

These half sections will wire these strong points on April 9/10th night. Wire will probably not be available for the wiring of the other two strong points till April 10/11th night.

23.   (a) 9th Division are carrying a cable forward to point H.13.b.45,[2] and from there it will be extended along communication trench south of the St. Laurent Blangy—Fampoux road to Athies, and eventually to Fampoux, by Brigade Signal Section.

(b) A trench wireless set will be sent forward and erected near the 3rd German system about H.14.b.64.[3]

(c) An amplifier will be sent forward and erected near the trench wireless set about H.14.b.64.

A power buzzer will be taken forward by the 1/King's Own. When Fampoux is captured it will be sent forward with its personnel to the 2/W. Riding Regt.

---

[1] These positions are within about 100 yards of the Green line and roughly equidistant from one another.
[2] Just west of the railway.   [3] Just north-west of Athies.

In order to avoid jamming instruments used by neighbouring brigades it will be used during the even five minutes only of the clock hours, i.e., 5 to 10, 15 to 20, etc.

(d) Two pigeons will be issued to each battalion and an extra two to the 2/W. Riding Regt. They will be distributed in the assembly area.

(e) Contact aeroplanes will receive signals by means of :—

    (i) Ground signal panels ;
    (ii) Lamps ;
    (iii) Flares.

Flares will be lighted in groups, one group to every 100 yards. They will be called for at Zero + 10.45 and Zero + 12 hours.

(f) Rockets and light signals will be used for communication with the artillery according to the following code :—

Succession of Green lights—Open fire.
Succession of White lights—Lengthen range.

Signals will be continued until the required response is made by the artillery.

The increment by which the range will be increased or decreased will be 100 yards.

Flags will also be used for indicating the position of the assaulting troops to the artillery. They must be waved, and not stuck in the ground.

(g) The brigade will establish a visual station on the Blue line about H.7.d.90.[1] As the advance continues an intermediate station will be established and manned by the 1/King's Own at about H.16.c.91.[2]

Battalions will arrange to maintain communication with one or other of these stations.

(h) There will be a divisional visual station in a house at G.23.c.52,[3] where messages will be received. No answers will be sent except " RD " or " G ".

24.   Prisoners will be sent by battalions to l'Abbayette, H.14.b.82, and taken over there by the A.P.M. 4th Division.

25.   Representatives of all units will report at Brigade H.Q. at 2 P.M. on April 8th and Zero + 4 hours April 9th to synchronize watches.

26.   Brigade H.Q. at Zero hour will be established in the assembly area, G.15.b and d.[4]

Before the brigade crosses the original British front line they will be established at G.17.a.70.45,[5] alongside the 26th Infantry Brigade H.Q. They will move later to the Blue line about H.13.b.89.

27.   Acknowledge.

Issued at 8.15 P.M.   J. F. L. FISON, Captain,
                                   Brigade Major,
                           12th Infantry Brigade.

[1] Near the point where the Arras—Douai road crosses the railway.
[2] Six hundred yards west of Fampoux.
[3] East of Arras, between the town and the cemetery.
[4] Between Ste. Catherine and St. Nicholas.
[5] East of the factory at St. Nicholas.

APPENDIX A
Time Table

Moves	Hours after Zero	Remarks
Leave assembly area	4.30	
Reach area behind Blue line . . .	6.40	
Leave Blue line	7.40	
Reach 3rd trench system W. of Brown line	8.40	
Pass over Brown line and move up to barrage	9.40 to 9.50	Exact
Reach 4th German trench system . .	10.12	
Advance from 4th German trench system	10.42	Exact
Reach Green line	11.18	

All times except those marked " Exact " are approximate.

APPENDIX B
Time Table of Creeping and Protective Barrages

Moves	Zero +	to	Zero +	Rate of Advance	Remarks
Protective barrage 300 yds. E. of Brown line	8.00		9.40	Stationary	
Advances till parallel to 4th German trench system	9.45		9.59	100 yds. per 2 mins.	Slower S. of F a m p o u x road
Advances along whole front and passes over 4th German system	9.50		10.17	100 yds. per 2 mins.	Smoke barrage also if wind permits
Barrage on the western edge of Fampoux and sunken road H.17.c.96 to H.11.a.6.3	10.17		10.19 to 10.21		
Lifts from sunken road and concentrates on the following localities :— Road junction, H.17.d.69, trench junction H.17.b.60.95, Hyderabad Redoubt	10.19 to 10.21		10.55		From 10.17 60-pdrs. enfilade the N. edge of Fampoux. This barrage lifts as far east as H.17.c.86 at 10.47, waits for the how. barrage, and then travels east with its most westerly line

	Zero + to Zero +		Rate of Advance	Remarks
Lifts off W. edge of Fampoux up to H.17.c.86	10.47			
Lifts from localities to protective positions beyond the Green line and remains on them	10.55	11.18	Stationary	After 11.18 a barrage (6″ how.) will be put down when called for only
Fampoux. Special double 6″ how. barrage 100 yds. E. of gun barrage	10.40	10.46	Stationary	
Advances through Fampoux	10.46	11.18	100 yds. per 2 mins.	
Lifts off the line from H.18.c.20 to H.18.a.22 and ceases fire	11.18			Will be put down on protective positions E. of Green line when called for only

BATTLES OF ARRAS

FIRST ARMY ORDER No. 104,
9TH APRIL 1917

1.   The Army Commander intends to consolidate the line gained
by Canadian Corps today, and to capture the objective on the
left where not reached today.

2. (a)   Canadian Corps will push out patrols towards Willerval
and Vimy with the object of occupying those places if
practicable.

(b)   Remainder of 9th Cavalry Brigade is placed under orders
of G.O.C. Canadian Corps, who will inform First Army if he
proposes to employ it.

(c)   Information received during today points to the possibility of German counter-attack on northern flank of
Canadian Corps. Canadian Corps reserves should, therefore, be disposed so as to deal with hostile movements from
the direction of Hirondelle Wood and Givenchy.

3. (a)   XIII. Corps will relieve infantry of XVII. Corps of Third
Army from right of Canadian Corps to Railway in B.27.A
on night of 11th/12th April under arrangements to be made
direct between Corps.

(b)   XIII. Corps will use roads shown in Map CN. 13 issued
with First Army Order No. 102 of the 3rd instant, and such
other roads as may be placed at their disposal by XVII.
Corps.

(c)   Instructions as to relief of artillery will be issued later.

(d)   XIII. Corps will assume command of front to be taken
over on completion of infantry relief, and will establish its
advanced headquarters at Ecoivres by 10 A.M. on morning
of 12th instant.

4. (a)   XIII. Corps will be prepared to move 63rd Division into
the area vacated by 2nd Division on receipt of orders from
Army Headquarters.

(b)   Following roads are allotted for this move :—
Bruay—Ourton—Dieval and
Houdain—La Comté.

(c)   Intervals of 500 yards will be maintained between
battalions.

(*d*)   Two battalions of 63rd Division, placed at disposal of I. Corps under First Army Order No. 103, remain at disposal of I. Corps.

5.   Acknowledge.

Adv. First Army.

J. BRIND,
Lt.-Col.
for
Major-General,
General Staff, First Army.

BATTLES OF ARRAS

TELEGRAPHIC ORDERS BY THIRD ARMY

Urgent Priority Operations.

VI. Corps, Fifth Army, G.H.Q., G.O.C.R.A., VII.
Corps, 3rd Bde. R.F.C., H.Q. Heavy Bde. M.G.C.,
XVII. Corps, XVIII. Corps, Cavalry Corps, 1st
Bde. Heavy Bde. M.G.C., Adv. First Army.

G.B. 885.   10th (April).

Corps are to reach the Green line at all points tomorrow with their
main bodies.   Outposts to be on the line Fontaine-lez-Croisilles,
Chérisy, Vis en Artois, Pelves, Plouvain, Greenland Hill.   Cavalry
Corps will move at 5 A.M. tomorrow and reconnoitre the Quéant—
Drocourt Line and will assist in the attack of the Fifth Army as the
situation permits.   VII. and VI. Corps will advance at 5 A.M. and
reach the Drocourt—Quéant Line.   Dividing line the Arras—Cambrai road, Guémappe, Vis en Artois to VI. Corps.   XVII. Corps
will move forward and consolidate Greenland Hill, Plouvain.

Third Army.   7.10 P.M.

BATTLES OF ARRAS

TELEGRAPHIC ORDERS BY THIRD ARMY

G.B. 936.   **11/4.**

The advance will be continued to-morrow. It is important that the pressure on enemy should be maintained in order to prevent enemy consolidating. Objective, the front Croisilles, Fontaine-lez-Croisilles, Chérisy, Vis en Artois, Pelves, Rœux Station and Chemical Works. Dividing line between VII. and VI. Corps, Arras—Cambrai road, Guémappe, Vis en Artois all to VI. Corps. Dividing line between VI. and XVII. Corps, River Scarpe. The most important direction is the front Chérisy, Vis en Artois, with a view to effecting a junction with the Fifth Army. Corps will arrange to support each other mutually during advance. The first operation will be (A) the capture of the high ground east of Wancourt, and (B) the capture of Rœux and the ground north of it. These operations will enable the flanks of VI. Corps to progress. Both these operations will be assisted by the artillery of the VI. Corps. Cavalry Corps will be ready to advance at two hours' notice.[1] Add'sd all concerned.

Third Army.   8.15 P.M.

[1] It was actually only half an hour after the despatch of this telegram that General Allenby sent the message mentioned on p. 273 ordering the Cavalry Corps back to the positions which it had occupied on the 8th April. (Compiler's note.)

BATTLES OF ARRAS

TELEGRAPHIC ORDERS BY THIRD ARMY

G.B. 962.   12/4.

The advance will be continued in accordance with No. G.B. 936 of yesterday, but Butt (XVII. Corps) will not advance and Hobbs (VII. Corps) while moving on Vis en Artois will form a flank on the Monchy le Preux—Boiry Notre Dame ridge.   Add'sd all concerned.

Third Army.   7.20 P.M.

BATTLES OF ARRAS

TELEGRAPHIC ORDERS BY THIRD ARMY

G.B. 990.   13/4.

The advance of Kelly (VI. Corps) and Hobbs (VII. Corps) will continue on 14th at 5.30 A.M. First objective generally the front T.6 central, 0.14 central, 0.2d, and thence down the spur to right of Butt (XVII. Corps).[1] Second objective track on left bank of Sensée, Chérisy village inclusive, copse in 0.21d,[2] St. Rohart Factory, Bois du Sart. Third objective occupation of bridgeheads on right bank of Sensée and occupation of Boiry Notre Dame. Dividing line between corps the Arras—Cambrai road, Guémappe and Vis en Artois to Hobbs (VII. Corps). Kelly (VI. Corps) will arrange to co-operate with Hobbs (VII. Corps) in the capture of Vis en Artois. Hours of advance from first and second objectives to be arranged between corps. Two tanks will co-operate if possible with each corps. Add'sd all concerned.

Third Army.   7.30 P.M.

[1] From the Hindenburg Line where the St. Martin—Fontaine road crossed it, to the enclosures on the Cambrai road three-quarters of a mile east of Guémappe, to Hill 100 (east of Monchy) and thence to the right of the XVII. Corps.

[2] Half a mile west of Vis en Artois.

BATTLES OF ARRAS

FIRST ARMY ORDER No. 108,
14TH APRIL 1917

1.   Information received points to the enemy holding the line
Rœux—Gavrelle—Oppy—Arleux en Gohelle—Acheville—Méricourt, and probably thence south of Siège No. 4 to Avion—Cité
de Moulin—Cité Ste. Elizabeth—Hill 70 (H.31.d).

2.   The Army Commander intends to attack the Gavrelle—Oppy
—Fresnoy line from the junction with Third Army to Acheville
inclusive, as soon as artillery can be got into position to cut wire
in front of it.
      G.O.sC. XIII. and Canadian Corps will report when they will
be in a position to carry out this operation.
      From Acheville (exclusive) Canadian Corps will refuse its
flank towards the Souchez river, keeping touch on its left with
the advance of the I. Corps.
      On the front north and west of Acheville, the advance of I.
and Canadian Corps will be restricted to keeping touch with the
enemy by patrols and seizing tactical points without engaging
infantry in serious fighting in the thickly populated area.

3.   Forward boundaries of Corps as under :—

Between XIII. and XVII. Corps (Third Army) :—
      An E. and W. line from Cross Roads H.4.b.86 (junction of
Blangy—Gavrelle and Fampoux—Bailleul roads) to southern
edge of Square Wood (I.2.c.99).

Between XIII. and Canadian Corps :—
      S.E. corner of Willerval to road junction at B.11.b.75 [1]—
south Corner of wood at C.1.a.31 [2]—Quarry, U.26.b.87.[3]
      (N.B. Arleux en Gohelle and Fresnoy inclusive to Canadian
Corps.)

Between Canadian Corps and I. Corps :—
      Souchez river to Liévin—Lens railway—Canal de la Haute
Deule.

          [1] Six hundred yards south of Arleux.
          [2] South of Fresnoy.
          [3] Two thousand yards east of Fresnoy.

4.   R.F.C. will take every opportunity of bombing Gavrelle—Oppy—Arleux en Gohelle—Acheville—Méricourt—Avion—Lens and Hénin Liétard.

5.   Acknowledge.

Adv. First Army.   W. H. ANDERSON,

8 P.M.   Major-General,

General Staff, First Army.

BATTLES OF ARRAS

THIRD ARMY ORDER No. 183,
20TH APRIL 1917

1.   The enemy in front of the Fifth, Third, and First Armies is
holding the general line Havrincourt—Quéant—Bullecourt—
Fontaine-lez-Croisilles—Rœux—Gavrelle—Oppy—Méricourt—
Lens, and thence to the original line.

2.   The First and Third Armies are to attack and secure the
general line U.13 central [1]—U.7 central [2]—T.6 central [3]—0.31
central [4]—Bois du Sart—Pelves—Greenland Hill—Gavrelle—
Oppy—Acheville, on the 23rd.[5]
      The Fifth Army is to support the right flank of the Third
Army with artillery fire.

3.   The Third Army will attack the enemy, the successive
objectives being shown on the map attached.   The infantry will
leave their original line at Zero and will reach the Blue line at
about Zero plus 1 hour.   The Blue line will be left at Zero plus
7 hours, and the Red line will be reached at Zero plus 7 hours
40 minutes.   On securing the Red line, a line of outposts will
be established east of it and the line itself will be consolidated.
Patrols will be sent forward towards the Green line so as to gain
ground towards it and obtain the necessary observation before
attacking it at a later date.   The subsidiary objectives of the
XVII. Corps are not shown.

4.   Dividing lines between Armies and Corps for the operation on
the 23rd are as follows :—
      (a) Between Fifth and Third Armies : Bullecourt—Quéant,
inclusive to the Fifth Army.
      (b) Between First and Third Armies : An east-and-west line
drawn from the cross roads in H.4.b06 to the southern edge of
Square Wood (I.2.b89).
      (c) Between VII. and VI. Corps : Guémappe—Vis en Artois—
Cambrai road to the VI. Corps.

[1] One thousand yards east of Croisilles.
[2] Six hundred yards south-west of Fontaine.
[3] Where the St. Martin—Fontaine road crossed the Hindenburg Line.
[4] One thousand yards west of Chérisy.
[5] Oppy and Acheville were subsequently deleted from the objective
of the First Army.

(*d*) Between VI. and XVII. Corps : the River Scarpe.

5.   All available tanks will be used, a proportion being detailed to operate north of the Scarpe.

Orders for the 1st Brigade, Heavy Branch, Machine-Gun Corps have been issued separately.

6.   Artillery instructions have been issued separately.

7.   Special Companies R.E. are distributed as follows :—

    XVII. Corps : 2 Projector Companies and 2 Sections of a Mortar Company ;

      VI. Corps : 1 Projector Company and 1 Section of a Mortar Company ;

     VII. Corps : 3 Sections of a Projector Company and 1 Section of a Mortar Company.

Gas from projectors will not be discharged between Zero – 6 hours and Zero.

8.   The 3rd Brigade R.F.C. will be employed as follows :—

(*a*) Squadrons under the Army.

Reconnaissances will be sent over the area Arras—Cambrai—Douai, to discover the movements of hostile reinforcements and delay their arrival by attacking them. Counter-battery and other areas, 4,000 yards beyond the front line will also be photographed.

(*b*) Under the Corps.

Squadrons will carry out artillery work, reconnaissances, and photograph within 4,000 yards of the front line.

Issued at 11 P.M.   L. J. Bols,
Major-General,
General Staff, Third Army.

BATTLES OF ARRAS

G.H.Q., O.A.D. 426

RECORD OF A CONFERENCE HELD AT NOYELLE VION AT 11 A.M. ON THE 30TH APRIL 1917

Present :

The Field-Marshal Commanding-in-Chief.
Lieut.-General Sir L. E. Kiggell, K.C.B. (C.G.S.).
Major-General J. F. N. Birch, C.B. (M.G.R.A., G.H.Q.).
Br.-General J. H. Davidson, C.B., D.S.O. (B.G.O.a., G.H.Q.).

General Sir H. S. Horne, K.C.B., Commanding First Army.
Major-General W. H. Anderson (M.G.G.S., First Army).

General Sir E. H. H. Allenby, K.C.B., Commanding Third Army.
Major-General L. J. Bols, C.B., D.S.O. (M.G.G.S., Third Army).

General Sir H. de la P. Gough, K.C.B., Commanding Fifth Army.
Major-General N. Malcolm, D.S.O. (M.G.G.S., Fifth Army).

The Field-Marshal Commanding-in-Chief reviewed the general situation. He stated that our action was dependent on that of our allies.

As regards the French, their losses had been heavy and they could not continue to operate by similar methods to those which they had employed since their main offensive was launched on the 16th April. There was a possibility of changes in the French higher command. This contingency would doubtless alter the military policy of the French, which would then probably be of a defensive nature with a tendency to avoid losses. Although the French War Minister and Prime Minister had given an assurance that offensive operations would be carried on, it was doubtful whether it was possible for the French Army to prosecute these on a large scale. The French higher command was now concentrating the efforts of the Armies on to certain important tactical points which it was necessary to secure. The French troops themselves are believed to be in good heart, but there is no reserve power behind them.

To sum up : Although it is by no means certain, it seems likely that the future policy of the French will be of a defensive nature, avoiding losses and awaiting the active assistance of America in the field.

As regards Italy, an offensive would be undertaken during the early part of May on the Isonzo and Carso fronts.

As regards Russia, reports were more favourable for an early offensive.

The Field-Marshal Commanding-in-Chief stated it was his intention to move steadily forward up to a good defensive line, and to consolidate it pending the development of the situation on the fronts of the whole theatre of war in Europe. It was hoped that this defensive line (which is described approximately in the paper O.A.D. 424, a copy of which is attached) should be reached about the middle of May. Once this line has been reached it will be possible to decide further action. It may then be necessary to continue on our present front, to attack on the Havrincourt front, or to shift the centre of gravity up to the Second Army. In the meantime it is necessary to hold the enemy and make him think that we are undertaking a methodical offensive similar to our operations last year on the Somme.

The Army Commanders present reviewed the situation on their own fronts. They agreed that the line mentioned in O.A.D. 424 was a suitable defensive line and that it coincided with their plans. They were all agreed as to the date of the next operation, viz., the 3rd instant.

The First Army Commander stated that he was short of troops and that he was anxious to capture Lens at an early date and so shorten his line. The enemy was no doubt expecting an attack in the neighbourhood of Lens. He was directed to submit to G.H.Q. a statement shewing his requirements in troops.

2.   The Field-Marshal Commanding-in-Chief drew the attention of Army Commanders to the following points :—

   (a)   The necessity for nursing Army Field Artillery Brigades. These Brigades do not form part of any Divisional or Corps organisation and therefore should be specially cared for by the H.Q. Staff of Armies.

   (b)   The necessity for the most careful study of any sector which is to form the objective of an attack. Not only should photographs of this particular part of the enemy's position be carefully examined for artillery and machine-gun emplacements, but as far as possible, the actual ground must be carefully compared with the results of these observations by the General Officer locally responsible for the execution of the attack.

   It will frequently be found that, owing to the great depth in which the hostile machine guns are now disposed, a simple moving " barrage " (i.e., a curtain of fire) will not suffice. On the contrary, a methodical combination of field and long-range heavy artillery fire will often be found necessary to prepare the ground for attack by infantry. And, to arrive at a thoroughly sound plan, it is more than ever necessary for Infantry Brigadiers and G.O.sC. Divisions to make the most careful study of our own gun positions with a view to an effective fire scheme in which guns of all classes (field, heavy, and trench) as well as machine guns, are carefully combined for a tactical objective.

(c)　　The action of machine guns in the attack requires further study. These may often be massed under Divisional control for some special purpose, such, for instance, as forming a barrage supplementary to the artillery barrage.

Advanced G.H.Q.　　　　　　　　　　　　　　L. E. KIGGELL,
1st May, 1917.　　　　　　　　　　　　　　　　　Lieut.-General,
　　　　　　　　　　　　　　　　　　　　Chief of the General Staff.

NOTE FOR CONFERENCE ON 30TH APRIL, 1917

Map 1 : 20,000

Preparatory to further operations, the Commander-in-Chief desires that the following general line may be gained by the First, Third, and Fifth Armies. The points mentioned are all inclusive.

First Army.　Hill 70 E. of Loos—Lens—Knoll in 22.c—Spur in 34 central—Eastern outskirts of Méricourt, Acheville, and Fresnoy—Knoll in C.1.b and d—thence just east of Oppy and Gavrelle.

Third Army.　(In co-operation with Fifth Army, as already arranged.)
Greenland Hill (8 central)—Hausa and Delbar woods —about 500 yds. east of Pelves—Keeling Copse—Bois du Vert—St. Rohart factory—wood in 21.c and d— Brickworks in 29.c—thence along ridge in a south-easterly direction through U.6.b and d, and thence along ridge to Riencourt.

The advance to this line should be deliberately and methodically made, without hurry. It will suffice if the line has been gained and consolidated by the 15th May.

The advisability of gaining Greenland Hill, Chemical Works, Rœux, and Pelves, by local operations before attempting any general advance to the line given above should be carefully considered by the Third Army Commander, as also the advisability of a preparatory operation to gain ground along the Hindenburg line on the right of the VII. Corps.

Army Commanders will report as soon as possible the successive steps they propose to take to carry out these instructions, and the date proposed for each step.

East of Quéant the Fifth and Fourth Armies will carry out any local operations they consider advisable, especially with the object of gaining improved artillery facilities for a further advance later, against the Hindenburg Line, on the front already selected at the conference held at Doullens on the 25th instant.

BATTLES OF ARRAS

SOME FIRST ARMY STATISTICS, BATTLE OF VIMY RIDGE

1. **Artillery.**
   Total of Guns and Hows.—covering attack   =1,100.
   ,,   ,,   ,,   —offensive & defensive =1,462.
   Extent of offensive front, about—3½ miles.
   Total tonnage of ammunition in front of Railheads on day of attack. } 40,300 tons or 109 B.G. trains of 32 wagons each.
   Greatest expenditure, 24 hours from noon to noon on day of attack, April 9th. } 7,200 tons or 22½ B.G. trains.

2. **Trains of Ammunition, Supplies, etc.**
   During preparatory period and during days of fighting—
   Trains per day for all purposes   =28 trains.
      (divided as follows)
   (a) Average daily tonnage of ammunition =2,960 tons or 8 trains.
   (b) Average daily tonnage of supplies   =3,600 tons or 9 trains.
   (c) Balance of trains coming into area carrying road stone, R.E. stores, Railway material, etc., etc.   =11 trains.

3. **Supplies accumulated before Advance, for whole of the First Army.**
   Strength of First Army—approximately—320,000 men.
                                                    75,000 horses.
   (a) In each of two Field Supply Depots there was stored = { 350,000 full day's rations for men. 75,000 full day's rations for horses.
   (b) In one special forward Field Supply Depot = { 50,000 full day's rations for men. 150,000 iron rations. 25,000 full day's rations for horses.
   (c) With each of two Corps in trenches =25,000 iron rations.

At each Supply Railhead—average = 3,000 full day's rations.

Collected in Supporting Points of each Corps =25,000 full day's rations.

Total Accumulation prior to Attack on April 9th.
Full day's ration for men   =828,000.
Iron Rations   =200,000.
Full day's ration for horses =100,000.

4. Railways.
Broad Gauge Railway extensions   = 10 miles.
Light Railway extensions, for fighting purposes, up to Sept. 1 from April 9th =120 miles.
Average weekly tonnage distributed by Light Railways, from Broad Gauge Railheads =34,000 tons.

5. Lorries, etc., in Service, on April 9th.
For Ammunition, Supplies, and various other purposes   = 4,600.
Motor Cycles   = 2,000.
Cars, including Ambulances   =   530.

6. Petrol Consumption.
Highest week during operations   =190,000 gallons.

7. Roads.
Mileage of roads which required repair and maintenance in the First Army zone—approximately =400 miles.
Mileage of new roads and of roads inside German lines made fit for traffic after April 9th = 100 miles (approx.).

8. Labour.
Employed in the Army, outside fighting troops, worked up to a maximum of =23,000.

9. Horses in the Army.   =80,000
Special arrangements for stabling and watering had to be made for these animals.

First Army,
5/10/17.

Printed in Great Britain by R. & R. CLARK, LIMITED, *Edinburgh*